The Nonprofit Board Answer Book

Have You Used These BoardSource Resources?

The Governance Series

Ten Basic Responsibilities of Nonprofit Boards
Financial Responsibilities of Nonprofit Boards
Structures and Practices of Nonprofit Boards
Fundraising Responsibilities of Nonprofit Boards
Legal Responsibilities of Nonprofit Boards
The Nonprofit Board's Role in Setting and Advancing the Mission
The Nonprofit Board's Role in Planning and Evaluation
How to Help Your Board Govern More and Manage Less
Leadership Roles in Nonprofit Governance

The Committee Series

Transforming Board Structure: Strategies for Committees and Task Forces
Governance Committee
Executive Committee
Financial Committees
Development Committee
Advisory Councils

Other Books

The Board Building Cycle: Nine Steps to Finding, Recruiting, and Engaging Nonprofit
   Board Members
The Board Chair Handbook
Chief Executive Succession Planning: The Board's Role in Securing Your
   Organization's Future
Dollars and Sense: The Nonprofit Board's Guide to Determining Chief
   Executive Compensation
Fearless Fundraising for Nonprofit Boards
Generating Buzz: Strategic Communications for Nonprofit Boards
Managing Conflicts of Interest: A Primer for Nonprofit Boards, Second Edition
Meet Smarter: A Guide to Better Nonprofit Board Meetings
Minding the Money: An Investment Guide for Nonprofit Board Members
The Nonprofit Board's Guide to Bylaws: Creating a Framework for
   Effective Governance
The Nonprofit Chief Executive's Ten Basic Responsibilities
The Nonprofit Legal Landscape
The Nonprofit Policy Sampler, Second Edition
The Source: Twelve Principles of Governance That Power Exceptional Boards
Taming the Troublesome Board Member
Understanding Nonprofit Financial Statements

Assessment Tools

Assessment of the Chief Executive: A Tool for Nonprofit Boards, Revised
Self-Assessment for Nonprofit Governing Boards

JB JOSSEY-BASS

The Nonprofit Board Answer Book

A Practical Guide for Board Members and Chief Executives

SECOND EDITION

BOARDSOURCE®
Building Effective Nonprofit Boards

John Wiley & Sons, Inc.

Published by Jossey-Bass
A Wiley Imprint
989 Market Street, San Francisco, CA 94103-1741   www.josseybass.com

Jossey-Bass books and products are available through most bookstores. To contact Jossey-Bass directly call our Customer Care Department within the U.S. at 800-956-7739, outside the U.S. at 317-572-3986, or fax 317-572-4002.

Jossey-Bass also publishes its books in a variety of electronic formats. Some content that appears in print may not be available in electronic books.

Library of Congress Cataloging-in-Publication Data
The nonprofit board answer book: a practical guide for board members and chief executives. 2nd ed.
        p. cm.
    Rev. ed. of: Nonprofit board answer book/by Robert C. Andringa, Ted W. Engstrom. Expanded ed. 2001.
    Includes index.
    ISBN 978-0-7879-9461-7 (cloth)
    1. Nonprofit organizations—Management. 2. Directors of corporations.
I. Andringa, Robert C. Nonprofit board answer book. II. BoardSource (Organization).
    HD62.6.A53 2007
    658.4'22—dc22
                                                                      2007011321

Printed in the United States of America
SECOND EDITION
HB Printing   10 9 8 7 6 5 4 3 2

BOARDSOURCE®

Building Effective Nonprofit Boards

BoardSource, formerly the National Center for Nonprofit Boards, is the premier resource for practical information, tools and best practices, training, and leadership development for board members of nonprofit organizations worldwide. Through its highly acclaimed programs and services, BoardSource enables organizations to fulfill their missions by helping build strong and effective nonprofit boards.

BoardSource provides assistance and resources to nonprofit leaders through workshops, training, and its extensive Web site, www.boardsource.org. A team of BoardSource governance consultants works directly with nonprofit leaders to design specialized solutions to meet organizations' needs. As the world's largest, most comprehensive publisher of materials on nonprofit governance, BoardSource offers a wide selection of books, videotapes, CDs, and online tools. BoardSource also hosts the BoardSource Leadership Forum, bringing together governance experts, board members, and chief executives of nonprofit organizations from around the world.

Created out of the nonprofit sector's critical need for governance guidance and expertise, BoardSource is a 501(c)(3) nonprofit organization that has provided practical solutions to nonprofit organizations of all sizes in diverse communities. In 2001, BoardSource changed its name from the National Center for Nonprofit Boards to better reflect its mission. Today, BoardSource has more than twelve thousand members and has served more than seventy-five thousand nonprofit leaders.

For more information, please visit our Web site, www.boardsource.org, e-mail us at mail@boardsource.org, or call us at 800-883-6262.

To Robert C. Andringa and the late Ted W. Engstrom,
who contributed their wisdom about nonprofit boards
in the previous edition of this book

Contents

Introduction: The World of Nonprofits

Nonprofit organizations are an essential part of our society. They struggle to reduce poverty and bring an end to homelessness. They strive to build safe places to learn and play, create inspiring art and music, and protect our natural resources. With more than 1.5 million organizations spending well over $1 trillion annually, the size and influence of the nonprofit sector make it imperative that nonprofit boards operate ethically, legally, and to their fullest potential.

One has only to look at the scandals of the day to see what happens when boards don't do what they're supposed to do. Nonprofit organizations face increased IRS scrutiny and more regulations from state attorneys general than other organizations. Legislation, however, only encourages boards to meet the basic fiduciary responsibilities for their organizations. Compliance is critical, but it isn't enough. Performance is equally essential. We need to find ways to help boards perform better so they, in turn, can help their organizations deliver on their missions.

As Peter Drucker said, "Management is doing things right; leadership is doing the right things." Boards need to add how they govern to that maxim. They need to invest time and energy in building collaborative relationships among board members and with the chief executive. Nonprofit chief executives provide a necessary voice in the boardroom, but they cannot carry out their duties without the full support of the board. In addition, board members need to be willing and able to think strategically, challenge ideas, and probe for better solutions. While they must bring independent thinking to decision making, they must do so collegially and with an eye toward inviting consensus. In the give and take in the boardroom, they must remember that governance is, fundamentally, a team sport.

From the Board Member's Perspective

Although a board is a team, it is composed of individual members, each with different but valuable abilities. Take a moment to ask yourself why you were recruited as a board member and what particular value you bring to your organization. Perhaps you have been an enthusiastic supporter of the organization's mission over the years, you have expertise in a particular area, you have proven fundraising abilities, or you are visible within the community.

Serving as a board member, however, goes far beyond fulfilling one or two specific functions. It also requires you to take a "big picture" approach to the organization, seeing it in new ways you may not have considered before. You'll be called on to think strategically and to make decisions that may effect the organization for years to come. In the process, you're likely to develop new skills that will make your tenure as a board member even more enjoyable and personally enriching. However, board service isn't just a hobby; it's a serious commitment of time, thought, and contribution.

By accepting the invitation to serve as a board member, you've entered the world of 501(c) organizations—the terminology used by the Internal Revenue Service to describe organizations that are exempt from paying federal income taxes because of the public benefits they provide. Typically, 501(c)(3)s are charitable organizations, 501(c)(4)s are social welfare organizations, and 501(c)(6)s are business-related organizations such as trade associations and professional membership societies. Generally speaking, these are all considered nonprofit organizations.

If you're familiar with corporate boards, you'll find some similarities—but many differences—between the for-profit and nonprofit worlds. Both for-profit and nonprofit organizations need strong board leadership and must adhere to certain legal principles that are outlined in state corporation laws. But for-profits answer primarily to their shareholders and focus on generating profits for those people. In contrast, nonprofits are accountable to their members, constituents, supporters, donors, and the public; their missions are not to make money but to make a difference in someone's life or the world.

From the Chief Executive's Perspective

The role of the nonprofit chief executive has evolved over the past century for a variety of reasons, including the growth and complexity of the nonprofit sector, the increasing professionalism and specialization of nonprofit employees, and other changes in the paid and volunteer work force. Furthermore, the responsibilities of chief executives vary widely depending on the organization's size, structure, and history. Yet, through time and across all nonprofits, there has been a common denominator: the chief executive works in partnership with the board.

An effective partnership between the chief executive and the board requires a delicate balance of power and authority. Finding and maintaining that balance is one of the central challenges of executive leadership. The chief executive provides leadership that engages and involves the board in governance. Together, the board and chief executive focus on the organization's mission, with both parties bringing their appropriate skills and expertise to bear for the desired results.

Common Questions, Practical Answers

Whether you're new to nonprofit boards or already have some experience in the nonprofit world, you're sure to have questions about the best way for your organization's board to function. That's where this comprehensive handbook will prove its value. In fact, the eighty questions answered in this book represent the queries that Board-Source most commonly receives, so you're sure to find information on whatever is on your mind these days. Most of the questions apply to all tax-exempt organizations that, by law, must have a governing board. Here and there, you'll find questions related to a specific type of organization. For example, most 501(c)(3) organizations engage in fundraising activities, but 501(c)(4) and 501(c)(6) organizations generally do not because they cannot receive tax-deductible donations. Conversely, a 501(c)(6) can engage in limited political activity, whereas a 501(c)(3) cannot.

Overview

In total, the book has seven parts. Each part builds upon the previous one, moving from general questions about nonprofit boards to more specific inquiries. Following is an overview of what you'll find in each section.

Part One: Basic Board Functions

Part One details the basic responsibilities one has when serving on a nonprofit board, plus the board's special role in various areas, such as strategic planning and fundraising.

Part Two: Board Structure

Part Two covers topics related to the board's internal organization, including the appointment of standing committees, the selection of board officers, and the key role played by the board chair.

Part Three: Selection and Development of Board Members

The third part provides much practical information on how to recruit, retain, evaluate, and engage board members so that both they and the organization benefit from their board service.

Part Four: Board and Committee Meetings

In Part Four, numerous strategies are offered for making the most of board members' time together, whether in the boardroom or on a retreat.

Part Five: The Board's Role as a Fiduciary

Part Five tackles the nitty-gritty details of safeguarding an organization's financial assets, such as the board's proper role in budgets, investments, and revenue generation.

Part Six: Board-Staff Relations

In Part Six, the various roles filled by staff members are clarified, with a special emphasis on the board's responsibility to select and adequately compensate the chief executive.

Part Seven: Organizational Change

The final part addresses issues that often arise as an organization matures, such as how to proceed after the founders are no longer involved with the organization and when to consider a strategic alliance or merger.

Board service is so multifaceted that it's difficult to compartmentalize the many areas it covers. The selection and development of board members (Part Three), for instance, influences how the board gets structured (Part Two). That's why, throughout the book, you'll find cross-references to related questions.

Content for Every Context

This second edition of *The Nonprofit Board Answer Book* expands upon the content in the first edition, which was written by Robert C. Andringa and Ted W. Engstrom and has been a perennial best-seller for BoardSource, having sold more than 22,000 copies. It also includes information from Andringa's follow-up book, *Answer Book II*, plus new material—all organized into a practical handbook written in a conversational style. BoardSource owes a debt of gratitude to these two authors for writing the first edition and for their role in promoting the book to a wide audience.

Think for a moment of the best conversations you've had with friends and colleagues. You were honest with one another—not shy about speaking up but relaxed, even if the topic being discussed was serious in nature. That's the type of conversation *The Nonprofit Board Answer Book* aims to have with you in the pages that follow. It follows a question-and-answer format, enabling you to quickly find an answer to a burning question you have right now. At the same time, it's easy to pick up and read straight through, either cover to cover or one section at a time.

At the end of each question-and-answer pairing, you'll find suggested action steps. These offer ways to put the information to a practical use on your own board and within your own nonprofit organization. Implementing some of these steps may lead to more questions as you become even more committed to fulfilling your responsibilities as a board member.

Remember: behind every good answer lies a good question. So keep asking those questions.

PART ONE

Basic Board Functions

Nonprofit organizations come in endless variations. They range from small, local homeless shelters to large, international trade associations; from community foundations operating within a geographic region to educational institutions that attract students from around the country. Their funding may come from just a handful of sources or from a wide array of charitable contributions, membership dues, government grants, fees from programs and services, and more.

Whatever their size, scope, or funding, however, all nonprofit organizations have a governing board composed of people who believe in and support the particular mission. As a member of a governing board, you have the pleasure—and the responsibility—of monitoring, overseeing, and providing direction for the organization's pursuit of that mission. Those responsibilities, which have legal ramifications, will call on you to develop or hone your skills in numerous areas, from financial management to organizational communication and from fundraising to strategic planning.

1.

What are the basic responsibilities of a nonprofit board?

If you could observe the board meetings of hundreds of nonprofit groups, you would be struck by how different they are in terms of structure, strength of leadership, working style, and relationship with the staff. But despite their diversity, all boards share the same basic duties.

Ten Basic Responsibilities of Nonprofit Boards

1. *Determine the organization's mission and purpose.* It is the board's responsibility to create and review a statement of mission and purpose that articulates the organization's goals, means, and primary constituents served (see Question 3).

2. *Select the chief executive.* Boards must reach consensus on the chief executive's responsibilities and undertake a careful

search-and-selection process to find the most qualified person for the job (see Question 70).

3. *Provide proper financial oversight.* The board may assist in developing the annual budget, regularly review financial statements, and ensure that proper financial controls are in place (see Questions 49 and 50).

4. *Ensure adequate resources.* One of the board's foremost responsibilities is to ensure that adequate financial resources exist for the organization to fulfill its mission (see Questions 8 and 47).

5. *Ensure legal and ethical integrity and maintain accountability.* The board is ultimately responsible for seeing that legal standards and ethical norms are respected (see Questions 7 and 52).

6. *Ensure effective organizational planning.* Boards must actively participate in an overall planning process and assist in implementing and monitoring the plan's goals (see Question 5).

7. *Recruit and orient new board members and assess board performance.* All boards have a responsibility to articulate prerequisites for candidates, orient new members, and periodically and comprehensively evaluate their own performance (see Questions 23, 28, 35, and 36).

8. *Enhance the organization's public standing.* The board should clearly articulate to the public the organization's mission, accomplishments, and goals and garner support from the community (see Question 10).

9. *Determine, monitor, and strengthen the organization's programs and services.* The board must determine which programs are consistent with the organization's mission and monitor their effectiveness (see Question 9).

10. *Support the chief executive and assess his or her performance.* The board should ensure that the chief executive has the moral and professional support he or she needs to further the goals of the organization (see Questions 63 and 64).

SUGGESTED ACTION STEPS

1. Board members, write down what you believe are the board's responsibilities. Consolidate the responses in a summary report for discussion at the next meeting. Try to reach consensus on the distinction between board and staff roles.

2. Board chair, invite a knowledgeable and objective volunteer to read the board's minutes from the past year and then observe two board meetings. Ask this person to summarize, based on his or her observations, the board's actual role (not what someone says it should be). You'll find out quickly whether or not the board is fulfilling its responsibilities.

2.

What are the attributes of a high-performing board?

With so many specific issues, documents, and decisions clamoring for their attention, board members rarely have the time to reflect on their overall role within the organization. To ensure the optimal performance of a nonprofit board, each member should understand and adopt the following "best practices" guidelines.

The role of the board is clear and distinct from the role of the staff. In a nutshell, the board's primary role is oversight and guidance; the staff's primary role is management.

Of course, the line between oversight and management can be fuzzy at times. The best approach is to see these two important roles as parallel and noncompeting. Everyone has the same goal in mind—fulfilling the organization's mission—and each has a specific role. Being clear about those goals paves the way for a smooth relationship between board and staff.

Board members have three "hats"—and only one can be worn at a time. These "hats" represent the three types of roles a board member can have within an organization: oversight, implementation, and volunteer.

The *oversight hat* is worn when the full board meets to make high-level decisions related to the organization's mission. The board, acting as a unified group rather than as separate individuals, sets the direction and then uses its authority to steer the organization on the appropriate course.

The *implementation hat* is worn when the individual board member has been granted specific authority to act on the full board's behalf. This typically involves a board delegating a task, such as helping to select which firm will conduct the next financial audit or directing the search for a new chief executive.

In most organizations, the board looks to the staff to implement its decisions. The same standard applies to tasks the board delegates to one of its members. When wearing their implementation hats, board members act as staff members would—they fulfill the task according to the board's directions.

The *volunteer hat* is always worn when board members serve as organizational volunteers—when they assist with operational details such as stuffing envelopes, writing articles, setting up and promoting events, raising funds, and so forth. When wearing this hat, they may be accountable to the chief executive, a staff member, or another volunteer. During these volunteer hours, board members must not try to take charge or run the program simply because they are board members.

The board is clear about the organization's stakeholders (those to whom it feels accountable) and its primary beneficiaries. Board members need to distinguish between the people who are stakeholders (for example, members, donors, or alumni) and those the organization serves (for example, students, families, or the community).

In some nonprofits, the stakeholders and the primary beneficiaries are one and the same. In trade associations, for example, the board is accountable to the members who pay dues, and the association's work also focuses on serving the same group.

The board provides clear direction. Through the guidelines it issues, the formal policies it adopts, and the official stands it takes on issues, the board delineates and communicates the organization's mission, purpose, and priorities. There should be no question about the organization's ultimate goals (see Question 3).

The chief executive is responsible for achieving goals within parameters established by the board. The board needs one person—the chief executive—to assume responsibility for getting the organization to where the board has determined it should be. When the lines of accountability are clear, no one can make excuses.

The chief executive often hires people to help fulfill those responsibilities, then holds them accountable in a management system that best fits his or her style (see Question 59).

The board chair manages the board with support from the chief executive. Every team, even one made up of all-stars, needs a leader. The board chair manages the board, and the chief executive manages the organization (see Question 19).

Research shows that higher-performing organizations have board-oriented chief executives. When the chair and the chief executive stick to their respective roles and provide mutual support to one another, the whole organization works better (see Question 20).

Committees serve the board's needs, not the staff's needs. Committees, with the assistance of staff, should speak to the board—not for it. Committees are useful only when they help the board do its work better. When not action-oriented, their primary job is to formulate good recommendations for board consideration (see Question 16). Task forces, which are designed for a specific purpose and then dissolved after the mission is accomplished, often offer an efficient alternative to committees.

Board meetings are well-planned. Meetings should include board-friendly materials sent in advance, concise agendas, clear results, and time for board fellowship. Advance preparation can make board meetings productive and enjoyable. Board members like to go home feeling that they made good, informed decisions that will advance the organization's mission (see Question 39).

Board members are carefully selected, oriented, and trained. It takes a deliberate effort to find people with the motivations, values, experience, and skills that will help the organization reach new levels of excellence (see Question 23).

High-performing boards provide orientation even before the elections, so candidates are not surprised or disappointed when they begin their jobs. Post-election orientation and ongoing board training keep board members focused on their contributions to organizational success (see Questions 27 and 28).

No matter how professional its staff is, a nonprofit organization depends on interested and engaged board members. That's why boards must also assume the responsibility for evaluating their own performance and developing strategies for improvement (see Questions 35 and 36).

SUGGESTED ACTION STEPS

1. Board chair, distribute these "best practices" for discussion at your next board meeting.

2. Board members, invite an informed volunteer to attend a full board meeting and several committee meetings; ask for an honest assessment of how well the board demonstrated its understanding of these statements.

3. Board chair, challenge each board member to develop a personal list of ten indicators of success for your board.

3.

What is the board's role and involvement in mission, vision, and values?

Successful nonprofit organizations use their mission statements as touchstones for everything board and staff members do. They ask, "Do the strategic plan and its supporting objectives build upon the whole reason we exist? Does the budget accurately reflect what's really important to us? Do our policies and procedures advance our purposes?"

A good mission statement articulates an organization's fundamental purpose. It helps focus the board members' thinking and actions on what distinguishes their organization from others. It should not so much describe the organization as define the results the organization seeks to achieve.

Ideally, a mission statement is succinct (fewer than thirty words), memorable, and clear-cut. Shorter statements can easily be printed and memorized by board members, staff members, and others. It serves as a reminder why the board and the staff commit themselves to the organization.

A mission statement is *not* a summary of strategies or programs. Here are some examples that illustrate the difference:

- *Yes:* We want to stimulate love of learning and reading in young people.
- *No:* Our mission is to provide free books to local schools.
- *Yes:* We want to strengthen our community by helping those who are in need gain self-sufficiency.
- *No:* Our mission is to operate neighborhood-based food banks and offer job training.

A *vision statement* differs from a mission statement yet also requires board approval. As its name implies, a vision statement paints a picture of what the organization sees possible in the future, often working with others having a similar vision but perhaps a different mission. Think of a vision statement as a long-term achievement that will guide the staff to fully realize the mission.

In its vision statement, a nonprofit organization will find its inspiration and motivation—what it wants to be or make happen in the future.

Typically longer than a mission statement, a good vision statement is both idealistic and realistic: it challenges people to accomplish something while making the accomplishment attainable. For example,

- We aspire to be the premier youth sports organization in the state, the first choice for boys and girls who want to develop their athletic talents to the best of their abilities in an atmosphere of caring and support.
- Our vision is to be the most effective voice and most vocal advocate for the preservation and restoration of wetlands throughout the world. We will operate in partnership with other like-minded organizations to shape the future of our world through research, science, and education.

- This organization is an agent for positive change and innovation within the health care field. We encourage and support the growth of healthy communities throughout the nation.

It's not uncommon for nonprofit organizations to revise their vision statements every five years or so, to reflect changes and developments in the world around them.

Many organizations also identify principles, corporate values, and other organizational goals.

SUGGESTED ACTION STEPS

1. Chief executive, post the mission statement and vision in a well-trafficked area, where board members, staff members, and visitors will be sure to see them.

2. Board members, to reinforce the organization's mission, consider reprinting the full mission statement (or highlighting three or four key words) on its letterhead.

3. Board chair, ask the chief executive to do reports tied to the mission statement, to make it measurable to some extent.

4.

When should an organization consider revising its mission statement?

There may come a time when your organization's mission statement no longer resonates with the people or community it serves, with donors, or with the world in general. That situation may be perfectly acceptable to the leaders of an organization intended to go out of business after achieving its goals. After all, why perpetuate a nonprofit organization named Fight the Interstate after the eight-lane highway has been built elsewhere and victory declared?

More often, a mission statement becomes outdated or downright obsolete, and leaders fail to realize it. The hints are probably there. Perhaps contributions have fallen off, media coverage is rare, registrations (and revenues) for long-popular events have decreased, volunteers are harder to find, or another group with more charisma has appeared on the scene. Something is not quite right, yet the usual fixes—stepping up public relations activities, tinkering with program content or delivery, revising the strategic plan—don't do the trick.

It might be time to reinvent the organization, or it might not (see Question 71). You may simply need to place a priority on building brand identity or making branding efforts consistent throughout the organization. You'll know only if you revisit your organization's purpose and reassess its future direction.

On a Mission

Why does your organization exist? Ask employees, board members, and other stakeholders that question, and you may be surprised at the variety of responses. Some people may not be able to clearly define the mission; others may be totally off the mark or talk about what is offered (products and services) rather than the *why* behind those offerings.

If confusion about your mission is widespread, you need to review why your organization was created in the first place. If those needs still exist, revising (or simply rephrasing) the mission can clarify the organization's bedrock values for all parties involved. Another possibility is to put more effort into clearly communicating your mission as it stands, assuming that it remains a valid statement of your organization's identity.

SUGGESTED ACTION STEPS

1. Board members, at least once a year, review the mission statement's relevance and discuss whether new laws, dramatic economic or environmental shifts, other organizations entering the picture, or other changes may justify a revision.

2. Board members, when conducting an organizational assessment or strategic planning session, include a review of the mission statement. Even if you don't change the mission statement, by keeping it top-of-mind you'll ensure that specific goals and objectives, as outlined in the strategic plan, flow directly from it.

3. Board chair, incorporate "mission moments" into board meetings. Set aside five minutes for board members to share how or where they saw someone or something effected by or in need of the organization's mission.

5.

What is the board's role in strategic planning?

As a board member, you must continually ask, What is our purpose? Who are we serving? How are we doing? Where are we going? Strategic planning is one way to sort out these questions.

Many people view strategic planning as the complicated, laborious task of producing a long document that often gets put on a shelf and ultimately has little influence on the organization. But planning is not just a product. It is a process that requires time, resources, patience, conflict resolution, persistence, and controversial choices. And it demands the full attention and involvement of the board, working in partnership with the staff.

The board sets the direction for the organization; on the basis of that direction, the staff fleshes out the plan, defines the strategies to achieve the plan, and determines the operational objectives. Undertaking the process of strategic planning offers numerous benefits to a nonprofit organization.

It maintains a mission-based focus. Organizations tend to wander from their stated missions over time, taking on new programs and serving new constituencies because money is available or new leaders want to do different things. Sometimes the mission statement is indistinguishable from that of other organizations, or it may seldom be referred to in decision making.

It offers a "reality check." Old methods may not meet the needs of today's environment. Assuming that certain problems—such as decreased fundraising, participation, or program quality—will correct themselves is a sure road to disaster. Strategic planning can identify emerging trends and new developments that the organization must address sooner rather than later.

It provides a performance review. Some nonprofits are good at doing things that no longer apply to their mission (or never did). A periodic review of actions will reveal which ones produce the best results, which are no longer significant, and where the majority of resources should be directed.

It builds consensus and ownership. It is not enough for the chief executive to have a clear picture of where the organization is going. All board members, staff, and constituents should agree on the organization's strategic direction. Consensus requires excellent communication and periodic consultation with a variety of people about how well the organization is doing and what it should be doing next.

It helps define leadership characteristics. Organizations go through cycles, each handled best by a leader who fits the times. Board members often hesitate to address the sensitive issue of whether and when a leadership change is needed for the challenges ahead (see Question 69). Strategic planning can help a board determine what the times require.

Process Questions

Once the rationale for strategic planning is clear, the chief executive typically looks at different models and proposes a specific process to follow. The proposal, which should be presented to the full board for approval, should address the following questions:

- *Who will lead the strategic planning process?* The chief executive usually fulfills this role, sometimes assisted by an outside consultant. Or the consultant or a particularly gifted board member might be best suited to take the lead.

- *What is the time frame?* Between six and nine months should be sufficient; if the process goes longer than that, the participants will grow weary of it. The board should receive interim reports.

- *Who will be involved?* The process should include board, staff, major donors, and other key stakeholders (perhaps community leaders).

- *What is the budget?* The process need not be expensive, but some direct expenses will be incurred.

- *What are the expected outcomes?* Be specific about reports, how relative priorities are to be identified, and whatever else the leadership expects from the process. For example, the board may require staff members to provide certain data that track actual results versus desired outcomes. This monitoring requirement forces critical analysis and creative reflection about new ways to achieve outcomes or prompts a reconsideration of the stated outcomes.

Strategic planning should flow from a clear mission—the reason the organization exists. What would the world lack if that mission were not pursued? Using the mission statement as a touchstone helps you decide whether to add or eliminate a particular goal or objective or a specific program. It helps you focus on what's really important when deciding what to do as an organization.

An extensive, months-long, formal process—complete with task forces, committees, and reports—may only be required every few years. But strategic thinking, learned and reinforced through the planning exercise, should become the continuous mode of thinking about all aspects of the organization. It's a state of mind that prevails whenever the board interacts and convenes, with potential priorities and future implications always being part of the discussion. In short,

- Strategic thinking is a continuous exercise, whereas strategic planning is a periodic one.
- Strategic thinking—an attribute of every high-performing board—involves consideration of today's issues and developments that may have an implication on tomorrow's activities.
- The goal of strategic thinking is not to predict the future but to anticipate it—by answering "What if . . .?" questions, exploring future scenarios, and identifying emerging trends.
- A board that thinks strategically creates a culture that focuses on critical issues, encourages the thorough exploration of ideas, and continuously aligns agenda items with organizational priorities.

SUGGESTED ACTION STEPS

1. Chief executive, if your organization has a strategic plan, familiarize the board with its contents.
2. Chief executive, if your organization doesn't have a plan, develop a proposal for undertaking a formal strategic planning effort.
3. Board members, have a short discussion about other experiences board members have had with strategic planning and what approach might be best for your organization.
4. Board members, brainstorm for an hour, listing the organization's strengths, weaknesses, opportunities, and threats

(SWOT analysis). Find out how well the board responds to thinking strategically by analyzing how the organization should take the SWOT results into account.

5. Board chair, ask board members to dream about what they would like the organization to do without regard for cost, energy, or time. These "dream sheets" can form the basis of a formal plan.

6.

What is the board's role in fundraising?

You have made a personal commitment to a nonprofit organization by agreeing to serve on its board. In addition to contributing your time and talents, that commitment should include providing financial support appropriate to your means and encouraging others to give as well. According to a survey conducted by BoardSource, more than half of the responding organizations require their board members to identify donors or solicit funds, attend fundraising events, and make a personal contribution.

As a board member, be prepared to do the following things.

Make a personal gift. Potential board members should be made aware of the organization's annual fundraising cycle and the expectation that they contribute. In fact, some organizations not only require specific contributions as a condition of board service but also charge each board member with raising a certain amount from others each year. When board members demonstrate their personal commitment by giving to an annual fund or capital campaign, it becomes easier to encourage others to follow suit (see Question 55).

During the year, the board should receive updates on the total goal set for donations from board members, progress toward that goal, and the percentage of board participation. Although "heavy hitters" are certainly welcome on a board, the amount contributed is less important than the participation rate. Foundations, government agencies, and individual donors will be impressed when your organization can report a 100 percent participation rate for board members.

Establish policies to guide fundraising. Fundraising policies, plans, and goals should be tied closely to mission, and it is up to the board to make sure this happens. Boards should not get carried away with details but provide wise direction for the staff.

When creating written policies to guide fundraising activities, consider the following questions:

- How much of the budget, now and in the future, should depend on outside giving?
- What is the maximum percentage of the budget that can be spent on fundraising?
- Should the organization apply for government grants or contracts?
- Are there fundraising strategies the board does not want staff members to pursue?
- What ethical standards should be followed?
- Does the gift acceptance policy provide a means for the board to decline a gift that either does not reflect the organization's mission or appears contradictory to it?

Select and encourage a development-savvy chief executive. Most chief executives spend a good deal of time raising money—but they can't do it alone. Board members can pitch in by offering time, advice, and contacts.

They can also encourage a chief executive to pursue education and training in this area. (For example, the Association of Fundraising Professionals offers a Certified Fundraising Executive, or CFRE, designation.) The board's affirmation of the chief executive—in fundraising as well as in other areas—sends positive signals to staff members and constituents and can often translate into fundraising success.

Recruit board members who are willing to raise funds. Each member brings to the board a unique network of contacts; tapping into these networks broadens your organization's fundraising base and raises awareness of the work it does. When identifying potential candidates, review the board's current composition and decide whether the organization needs more board members with talents and experience in fundraising or members who are well-connected to potential sources of funds. Be straightforward about recruiting prospective members who will be especially effective in this area (see Question 23).

Volunteer to help. All board members have a place in fundraising. If directly asking for contributions isn't your strong suit, volunteer to take on other tasks. You might, for example, host a luncheon, sell tickets to an event, sign or send letters to people you know, or make thank-you calls to donors. Board members who are not major donors can still support fundraising efforts by attending events and bringing a positive attitude to all donor interactions and initiatives.

Evaluate your efforts. Staff members can be too close to the fundraising process to evaluate the results objectively; approaches that work well at first may be continued far beyond their effectiveness. Through regular yet informal evaluation, you and other board members can determine the cost-effectiveness of various events or activities. Also, as a contributor yourself, you're in a good position to offer feedback on which fundraising strategies appeal most to a particular segment of the community.

SUGGESTED ACTION STEPS

1. Board members, ask staff members to give a board presentation on current fundraising efforts, including an analysis of results and recommendations.

2. Board members, if you don't have one already, recommend a simple policy that says, "Each board member is expected to be a donor every year."

3. Board members, develop guidelines for the organization's fundraising efforts, including a gift acceptance policy.

7.

What are the legal duties of a board member?

From a legal standpoint, trustees, officers, or board members of a nonprofit board are held to these three standards:

- *Duty of care.* This refers to board members' responsibility to actively participate in making decisions on behalf of the organization and to exercise their best judgment while doing so.
- *Duty of loyalty.* When acting on behalf of the organization in a decision-making capacity, board members must set aside their own personal and professional interests. The organization's needs come first.
- *Duty of obedience.* Board members bear the legal responsibility of ensuring that the organization remains true to its mission and purpose by its compliance with all applicable federal and state laws.

As an example of a legal issue, organizations designated as tax-exempt under Section 501(c)(3) of the Internal Revenue Code may not engage in excessive lobbying and may not make contributions to certain types of organizations, such as political campaigns. If the organization does not operate in accordance with these restrictions, it may have to pay a stiff fine or may even lose its tax-exempt status (see Question 76).

The Internal Revenue Service (IRS) can also penalize individuals who take advantage of their positions inside nonprofits. Known as intermediate sanctions, these penalties apply to "excess benefit" transactions between a nonprofit organization and disqualified persons. "Excess benefit" simply refers to any transaction that exceeds fair market value for the benefit received by the nonprofit or is not comparable to what similar organizations or companies pay for a similar product or service. Any financial transaction is subject to scrutiny, from severance payments to transfers of property to officers' liability premiums.

According to the IRS, the term *disqualified person* refers to anyone in a position to exercise substantial influence over the affairs of the nonprofit organization within the preceding five years. This category would include officers, directors, high-level employees (including department managers), major donors to the organization, and even the families of all these types of people.

Should the IRS determine that a disqualified person has received an excess benefit, the person has a tax liability of 25 percent of the excess amount. (If the tax is not paid or the excess amount not returned to the organization within a specified amount of time, the penalty increases to 200 percent.) In addition, any board member or manager who knew of or approved the transaction is subject to a 10 percent tax on the excess amount (up to a maximum of $10,000 per excess-benefit transaction). The IRS may waive the taxes and penalties should the nonprofit organization uncover the excess-benefit transaction and correct it before an IRS audit takes place.

Intermediate sanctions are applicable to 501(c)(3) organizations—excluding private foundations—and 501(c)(4) organizations. To protect itself from intermediate sanctions, a board should be sure to fulfill the three requirements of the "safe harbor" provision; this applies when nonprofit boards are determining the chief executive's compensation or engaging in a financial transaction with a disqualified person. The safe harbor requires the board to

1. Approve the transaction, with the interested person not present during the debate and not casting a vote.

2. Obtain and review comparability data related to the transaction.

3. Document the basis for its decision.

SUGGESTED ACTION STEPS

1. Board members, make sure the board has a written policy that either prohibits board members from engaging in business or financial transactions with anyone directly connected to the organization or clearly states conditions under which such actions are acceptable.

2. Board chair, set aside time during a board meeting to review the restrictions that accompany the organization's tax-exempt status.

3. Board chair, use the three legal duties of a board member as a discussion topic during a board development session or leadership retreat.

Q&A

8.

What is the board's role in financial management?

The level of financial detail board members receive can be confusing to the layperson. For this reason, many boards recruit a few members who understand the intricacies of budgets, investments, audits, and financial reporting. These board members typically are assigned to the financial committees.

Still, every board member must take finances seriously. A board member has a fiduciary duty for the organization, a responsibility to see that the organization is well-managed and that all the finances are safely guarded. In general, these three areas require your attention and participation.

* *Policies.* Every board should have organized financial policies, written in language everyone understands, that provide guidance to the staff. These policies spell out the board's desires regarding matters such as controls on cash receipts and disbursements, budget practices, investments, operating reserves, capital budgets, risk management, financial reports, and au-

dits. In short, these policies ensure that the finances of the organization are professionally handled.

- *Budget.* Even with strong financial policies in place, all nonprofit boards must see and approve the annual budget. Budget discussions often bring out critical assumptions and policy matters that might be overlooked. Because revenues and expenditures can shift frequently throughout the year, budget policies should define the staff's flexibility to move funds within or between budget categories. It is common to have a mid-year budgetary review and make some adjustments— even if the original budget was as realistic as possible (see Question 49).

- *Financial Reports.* The board should understand the various financial statements nonprofits use, then clarify what reports it wants and when. The typical reports are statements of financial position, statements of financial activities, and statements of cash flow. Staff members often supplement these reports with graphics, trend data, comparison data with similar organizations, and adequate commentary to highlight significant budget variances.

More specifically, in its role as the organization's financial monitor, the board must ensure that the organization

- Keeps accurate and up-to-date financial records
- Prepares and follows an annual budget
- Prepares accurate and timely financial statements
- Effectively manages assets
- Follows established investment policies
- Complies with federal, state, and local regulations and applicable reporting requirements
- Conducts an annual external financial audit

- Conducts audits or prepares reports required by the government or other funders
- Has internal controls in place for staff and board members who deal with finances to ensure segregation of duties
- Effectively manages risk through the purchase of insurance policies and the establishment of conflict-of-interest policies

Good Questions

Even if you're not a financial expert, you can ask good questions about all the figures, columns, and statistics you see. For example,

- Do we have adequate reserves should we unexpectedly lose major funding?
- Do we actually put money in the budget for the required depreciation expenses in case we need a new roof?
- What percentage of our total expenditures goes for staff compensation and benefits, and how does that compare with similar organizations?
- How might moving a major revenue-producing event or fundraising initiative to a different time of year have an effect on the organization's cash flow?
- Would the revenue from our potential business partnership require us to pay unrelated business income taxes?

Questions about the financial reports often prompt discussions that lead to revised policies, better ways to present the budget, or new reports that allow the board to draw a more complete picture of the prevailing financial situation.

SUGGESTED ACTION STEPS

1. Board members, answer this question on a blank index card and give the card to the chair to use in evaluating the need for further training: "On a scale of 1 to 10, how satisfied are you that you understand our finances?"

2. Board chair, ask a CPA or auditor who works with nonprofit organizations to make a board presentation on this topic.

3. Board members, if you do not have written board policies to guide the staff in all areas of finance, discuss who should work with the chief executive and the chief financial officer to draft them.

9.

What is the board's role
in organizational evaluation?

To be effective monitors, board members need to receive—and read—brief written summaries prepared by the staff. These periodic reports, often provided quarterly and in conjunction with the materials for an upcoming board meeting, should track the organization's progress toward its strategic goals by including key activities, accomplishments, and results. In the area of finances, for example, the quarterly update from the chief executive might report, "We are 10 percent over budgeted revenues and 6 percent under budgeted expenditures. With donor income about the same as the last three years at this point, we project ending the year with $40,000 to $50,000 more in net reserves than planned. It is a good year financially."

This short report can be accompanied by copies of more detailed financial reports, the current budget, and financial statements that support the overall analysis. Although only a few people may delve into all the details, good stewardship and good governance require that all board members have access to complete information about the organization's financial status. Board members who serve on the finance committee can assist their colleagues by explaining terms and concepts, providing additional details on the organization's financial situation, and answering questions during the meeting.

Evaluating Priorities

Should they desire to know more about a particular area, board members should have no qualms about asking staff members or members of the finance committee to provide more details or a fuller explanation. In fact, "Why?" is a good question to pose in regard to any program, product, service, or activity.

In keeping with the board's role, this question must have a strategic focus rather than an operational one. For example, it is certainly appropriate for a board member to ask the chief executive, "Why do you believe revenues from that activity are down this year, compared with last year?" But asking, "Why didn't you have more staff members selling tickets?" oversteps the board's role (see Question 2).

Periodically, often in conjunction with the strategic planning process (see Question 5), board members should familiarize themselves with the products and services offered by the organization. Do they appear to fit the organization's current goals and priorities—or are they possibly pulling the organization away from something else it should be doing? Many activities get started because they were the right thing to do at the time. But times change. And some programs and services might have been launched simply because they were pet projects of leaders in years past.

Without the pressures of the marketplace, which prompt for-profit organizations to continually evaluate their offerings, nonprofits tend to perpetuate programs from one year to the next. Only a financial crisis or perhaps a leadership transition prods most nonprofits into taking a good look at the value of everything they offer. Yet money could be saved—or an even better program could be developed—if program evaluation were integrated into the board's strategic planning cycle.

Board members must answer to stakeholders about how wisely a group's resources are being employed and deployed.

When adequate professional staff does not exist to provide comprehensive reports, consider appointing an evaluation team, consisting of volunteers and a staff liaison, to look at each program, gather relevant data, and ask the following questions:

- How does this program relate to our mission?
- When was it started?
- What were the program's initial goals? Have those goals changed over time?
- What is the annual budget?
- What is the cost per member, client, or customer served?
- Why should we continue to do this? What are the tangible and intangible benefits?
- How successful is the program at meeting its goals?
- Is there another way we might achieve the same goals?
- What value does this program have in relation to the others? Where on the list does it rank?
- If this program should be continued, how might it be improved or combined with another initiative? What are the financial and staffing implications of those changes?
- If this program should be discontinued, what are the implications? What exit strategy should we employ (for example, phase it out or cease immediately)?

When all is said and done, the public holds the governing board accountable for getting the job done ethically, efficiently, and effectively. As a result, board members must be willing to say no to a project, a program, an initiative, a donor, a staff member, or even another board member with the potential to pull the organization away from its core values and purpose.

SUGGESTED ACTION STEPS

1. Board members, periodically review all of the organization's initiatives and activities to ensure that they remain relevant and necessary.

2. Board members, develop a form to make the evaluation process as consistent as possible for the board and staff members undertaking it.

10.

How should the board connect and communicate with constituents?

As a board member, to whom are you accountable? Every board should identify and define its stakeholders—who are not necessarily the same people as the primary beneficiaries of a nonprofit's work. For example, in most membership organizations, the stakeholders and the primary beneficiaries are the same: the dues-paying members. For a school board, however, the stakeholders would usually be parents and taxpayers, whereas the primary beneficiaries are the students.

Effective boards form links with all of their constituencies. As a board member, you should always be knowledgeable enough about the organization to represent it at events it sponsors, at meetings with funders, in interactions with constituents, and within the community in general. Following are some reasons why:

- Board members who are well-informed help build loyalty and confidence in the organization's mission.

- Donors need assurance about an organization's financial stability, its strategic direction, and its wise use of their contributions. The board chair might do this by writing a message in a newsletter or magazine or by signing a letter that accompanies the annual report of finances and activities.

- Various constituencies may be confused or concerned about a decision to significantly change the organization's structure or operations, such as through a merger with another organization. Having made the decision, board members are in the best position to explain the strategic advantages (and their thought processes).

- Whenever a surprise change in leadership occurs, such as the unexpected resignation or termination of the chief executive, the board can quickly put rumors to rest by being the official source of information on what occurred and how the leadership transition will be handled. The communication should be timely, forthright, courteous, and assuring. In general, any matter dealing with the chief executive is most appropriately communicated by the board.

Of course, the board doesn't simply communicate in one direction. For a true dialogue to occur, board members must listen to various constituencies as well as speak to them. Although the board chair most often makes any public statements on behalf of the board, all board members should agree upon and participate in other efforts to link with the people or community represented or served, for example, when the following occur:

- The board is contemplating a revision or shift in the organization's mission. Sending a survey from the board to significant constituencies will not only obtain grassroots input but also create additional support. Survey recipients will know that any major change would be the result of serious deliberation by the board.

- The organization wishes to improve its services to its many members, who are geographically dispersed, by holding hearings in each membership region. The chief executive and several board members might attend each hearing, a strategy that emphasizes the board's willingness to hear supporters' concerns and ideas.

- A nonprofit prepares several board members ahead of time to appear on or cohost a local radio or television show that will boost the organization's visibility and educate the community on its mission.

- The board invites one or two of the constituents it serves or represents to a dinner preceding the board meeting. Listening to the personal stories of those served can dramatically boost board members' understanding of the mission.

The public profile of boards varies greatly. Some organizations achieve visibility and credibility mostly by having well-known people on the board. These organizations usually list board members' names on their letterheads and in their publications. Other boards prefer to keep a low profile.

Whatever their visibility within the community, board members should always inform the chief executive of their participation in or attendance at events. The chief executive should even have the opportunity to veto an idea. After all, he or she interacts constantly with the external constituency and should not be put in the position of having to explain a board initiative that he or she did not understand or support.

SUGGESTED ACTION STEPS

1. Board chair, invite board members to reflect on the last time they linked directly with the organization's constituency.

2. Board members, list the constituencies—current and prospective—the board should listen to as it plans for the future.

3. Chief executive, develop an "elevator speech"—a short statement (two or three sentences) of what the organization does—and give it to board members so that they can be prepared to deliver it at any time, to anyone who asks.

4. Board members, attend and participate in community events sponsored by the organization, to publicly reaffirm your commitment to its mission.

11. $\mathcal{Q}\mathcal{A}$

How does a board
function as a team?

High-performing boards confirm the theory that the whole is stronger and more effective than the individual parts. Take a diverse group of people, all of whom have strong individual talents, and put them on the same board. They will accomplish more together, by combining their ideas, experience, and expertise—by playing off of one another's strengths and expanding their own thinking in the process.

Of course, the dynamics of any group situation can sour, no matter how well-intentioned the participants. Some people are naturally outspoken and may unknowingly silence board members who are more introspective. Some come to decisions by talking through, and perhaps arguing about, various options with the whole group; their colleagues on the board may have a less-combative style and prefer to process information individually or in small groups. A skillful chair is able to involve each member in board work regardless of personal styles and attributes.

Following are some ways to keep your board functioning well as a team.

Focus on the mission. No matter what their personalities or approaches, all board members should share one characteristic: they must be committed to the organization's mission. They may disagree on many other things about the organization, but its reason for being should be a rallying point and a touchstone for decision making.

Build a culture of trust. The group dynamics of a board continually change, depending on who attends or misses a particular meeting and which members are completing or starting terms. No matter who is coming and going, however, board members must know they can count on one another—to complete an assignment, to engage in decision-making discussions, to review information thoroughly before voting, to aim for the same goals as an organization.

This culture of trust is rooted in respect, integrity, and accountability and built through the frequent communication of expectations and appropriate roles. Board members must hold their colleagues accountable for ethical behavior, such as maintaining confidentiality on certain topics and fully disclosing any potential conflicts of interest. They must be willing to remind one another of the board's role, pointing out, for example, when a colleague strays into operational issues that are the chief executive's responsibility.

New board members will sense the high level of trust that exists and instinctively conform to that culture. Also, political factions that can break apart boards have no breeding ground when all board members deal openly with one another.

Speak your mind. Even on a high-performing board, not all members will agree with every decision. But all should feel comfortable— within the board's social and cultural environment—to respectfully disagree with the direction a discussion or decision is headed.

As the facilitator of board discussions, the chair has the primary responsibility for ensuring that everyone has the opportunity to ask questions and speak about an issue before voting. Even without the invitation, however, you as a board member have the personal responsibility to speak frankly if you are troubled or uncomfortable about a strategy or policy decision. You may think that no one feels the same way you do, yet by breaking your silence you may discover otherwise. Then others might feel more comfortable sharing their dissenting opinions—and the organization might avoid making a decision that would have negative consequences.

SUGGESTED ACTION STEPS

1. Board members, consider developing a code of ethics, or a statement of standards of behavior, for board members to affirm in writing each year.

2. Board chair, invite an expert in group dynamics to observe several board meetings and provide an objective critique of how the board could work together better as a team.

12.

How does the board avoid the extremes of "rubber stamping" and micromanaging?

A board member provides oversight and guidance, always keeping in mind the organization's mission. That doesn't mean approving, without question, every program, project, and budget proposed by staff. Nor does it mean becoming engrossed in operational details such as deciding which flowers are planted by the front door.

Board members who are clear about their responsibilities are much less likely to become involved inappropriately in administration or to distance themselves from critical decisions (see Question 1). Strive for balance.

"Rubber Stamping" Signs and Solutions

Being a "rubber stamp"—approving, without question, whatever staff members or committees recommend—often starts with a decline in the number of full board meetings and increases in the number of committees and committee meetings. Board members may feel somewhat informed about their committee areas of responsibility but don't believe that full board meetings provide enough time to be informed about other areas. They begin to see themselves more as advisers to rather than members of the governing body. Or they may feel that their individual contributions are not essential to the full board's work—a common reaction when the board is too large or when an executive committee takes on greater responsibilities (see Questions 13 and 17).

To avoid being a rubber stamp, read the background materials on an issue, analyze the statistics, listen carefully to presentations, and ask pointed questions about stakeholders' needs, relevance to mission, and success (or failure) of strategies. Put everything to the test, even if something is presented or recommended by a high-profile board member you admire, a long-serving staff member, or even the founder of the organization.

Your opinion counts, too. Remember that you have legal, ethical, and moral responsibilities, all of which should overshadow any belief that you should keep silent if something troubles you (see Question 7). In fact, the board culture should welcome open debate and discussion with the caveat that any decision the board makes should be publicly supported by all of its members, even those who personally disagree.

If you reach the point where you don't feel you have time to attend meetings or read board materials thoroughly, do the right thing by resigning. Then the organization can appoint someone better able to fulfill the myriad responsibilities of board service.

Micromanagement Symptoms and Cures

Some board members have a great familiarity with programs and services that other board members recognize only as a line in a budget. They may know employees by name, especially in organizations with a small staff. Given their grassroots expertise, these board members can bring invaluable insights to board discussions, provided they know when to take off the volunteer hat and put on the governance hat (see Question 2).

How do you know when board members have crossed the line and begun to micromanage? When they, while functioning in the role of a board member, exhibit such behaviors as

- Offering unsolicited opinions on purchases of office equipment or selection of vendors
- Becoming involved in personnel issues, such as hiring and firing staff (other than the chief executive) or approving individual salary increases
- Demanding to review invoices and receipts
- Creating a committee that deals with operational issues already assigned to staff members
- Sitting in, uninvited, on staff meetings

Although it's certainly appropriate for a board to make the decision on where the organization's new office will be located, it's not appropriate for the board to select the office decor or design the sign for the front door. Likewise, the board's responsibilities include approving budgets for specific programs; they do not include proofreading the marketing materials or deciding what will be served for lunch during the meeting. The board's work, which usually includes serving on a committee or two, leaves no time for participating in staff decisions. Staff members should understand the role of board members as well, so they don't unwittingly ask questions or provide the kinds of information that pull governance volunteers into management functions.

The board chair and chief executive together should review the agendas for board meetings to ensure that they do not unwittingly promote micromanagement. Topics should relate to strategic goals, not administrative issues. Supporting materials should present high-level information that facilitates discussion.

If a board member veers toward micromanagement, the board chair can instead steer that person toward an assignment related to the area of greatest interest. For example, a board member who often asks detailed questions about the organization's hardware, software, and computing capabilities would be a prime candidate for an operational task force to investigate and assess needs for upgrading and maintaining the information technology system. Another option is to give the person a challenge outside his or her comfort zone, such as helping develop a long-range plan, to channel energy and attention away from operations and toward strategic direction.

Of course, a hands-on approach by the board may be warranted in a crisis or transition situation, such as when the chief executive has resigned. However, this means of maintaining continuity must end when a new chief executive has been hired (see Question 59).

The best way to keep micromanagement in check is to prevent it from ever taking hold. Clarifying the distinct roles of staff and board members during the board orientation may reduce the potential for micromanagement by board members. Note that just because they can do something doesn't mean they should.

SUGGESTED ACTION STEPS

1. Chief executive, when developing agendas and advance materials for board meetings, make sure they do not emphasize operational issues or open the door to discussions of minutiae.

2. Board chair, keep board members focused on their governance responsibilities by incorporating board development or educational activities into meetings, such as presentations by guest experts or constituents.

PART TWO

Board Structure

A board has the latitude to decide which governance structure works best for the organization's mission, activities, culture, and preferred way of working. Some boards, for example, have no committees. Most find it helpful to have a few committees and task forces, sometimes supplemented by advisory councils.

The best structure for your board is the one that brings organization to its activities and promotes efficiency in the process. As times change and different challenges arise, the board structure may need to change, too. Well-organized boards, above all, are streamlined—they do not duplicate others' work or complicate processes unnecessarily.

QA

13.

What is the best
size for our board?

There's no magic number that guarantees board engagement, efficiency, and productivity. The answer depends on the organization's culture, the nature of its mission, the experience and expertise of board members, and the board work that must be accomplished.

The smaller the board, the easier it can be to schedule in-person meetings and get a quorum, especially if all board members live close by. For instance, it probably won't take long for a five-member board to look at calendars and agree to meet only when all members are available. That is much harder to do with a board of thirty. In contrast, a larger board brings a greater breadth and depth of experience to the organization and can "share the load" so that individual board members do not become overwhelmed by their responsibilities and therefore risk burnout.

From a legal perspective, each state determines the minimum number of board members required to comply with its statutes on nonprofit corporations. No states require more than three board members, yet many organizations recognize that the minimum legal limits are not necessarily the best size for them. Many boards number in the twenties or even the thirties. According to BoardSource research, the national average for a nonprofit board is seventeen members.

Merits of Size

The smaller the board, the easier it may be for the chief executive and key staff members to stay in close communication with and learn what motivates individual board members. There may be a greater sense of camaraderie and engagement because board members have the opportunity to get to know one another well, and the board may govern less formally.

People who serve on a small board may have a heightened sense of loyalty that translates into more personal involvement; they know they'll be missed if absent from a board meeting. Feeling essential to the board's work can increase a board member's satisfaction and deepen his or her personal commitment to the organization. Also, a small board is more feasible if you invite people from outside the board to serve on advisory groups, ad hoc task forces, or board committees. As an added bonus, having fewer members makes the chair's job of managing the board a bit easier.

Organizations with many members or a diverse constituency may have a political reason for having a large board—for example, to properly reflect the needs of all geographic areas or all types of stakeholders. Larger boards need to be more disciplined about establishing—and following—written policies and procedures to guide their work. And the more board members there are, the greater the number of people who can be effective in fundraising and community outreach efforts—but only when wearing their volunteer hats (see Question 2).

Typically, larger boards create executive committees—a smaller group within the board usually composed of the organization's officers and other key leaders. Because this smaller group (perhaps five or six people) is easier to convene and communicate with, it may, over time, take on policymaking responsibilities that rightfully belong to the full board. The danger in this scenario is that the full board may not feel its input is necessary or desired; it may become tempted to refer tough issues to the executive committee for action (see Question 17).

Of course, smaller boards will incur fewer costs than their larger counterparts. The costs associated with recruiting, training, convening, communicating with, and sustaining larger boards can be substantial, especially if the organization offers to pay travel expenses.

The question of board size is a complicated one to answer and requires a careful analysis of the individual situation. Do not simply rely on tradition ("We've always had forty-two board members") and automatically assume that the current size of the board is optimal for the organization's strategic priorities. Put the issue on the table now and then. As in other areas, periodically evaluating the size and composition of the board may lead to better practices.

SUGGESTED ACTION STEPS

1. Board members, make a list of how you think your board would function differently if it were half the size. How about twice the size?

2. Board members, discuss possible reasons for inefficiency other than a board's size.

3. Board chair, take a confidential poll of your board members: ask what the ideal size of the board should be and whether the board should consider changing its size.

4. Board members, benchmark similar organizations and compare the sizes of their governing boards.

14.

How should we structure our board?

Many boards have enough capable people, a good mission statement, and other elements for success. But when an inefficient structure is perpetuated, board members become discouraged and their interest wanes.

Let's say a board has forty-five members with no term limits. The board chair has served for twenty-nine years; he was one of the founders, and people hope he will leave much of his estate to the organization when he dies. Although new committees have been created to address major issues, they have no written job descriptions and tend to remain in existence far beyond their usefulness. Committee effectiveness depends on who is appointed committee chair. Some board members serve on three committees, while others don't serve on committees at all. A handful of board members never miss a meeting; the majority attends board meetings on occasion. In short, this model does not engender participation or new ideas.

Fortunately, board structure is one of the easiest things to create, maintain, and repair when necessary. It all starts with the organization's bylaws, which should outline the basic structure of board operations (including how the board chair is selected, how long he or she may serve, the range of how many members may serve on the board at one time, and so forth). The bylaws are not a sacred document; they should be changed whenever the majority of board members think the board can be structured more efficiently or productively.

The board leadership's willingness and ability to make a structure work is more important than following a textbook definition. The following suggestions can help you reconsider or refine your board's current structure.

- Evaluate your structure every couple of years. Change it if 70 to 80 percent of board members favor a specific revision. Tradition has its value—but not if it discourages board members from engaging actively in board work.

- Ensure that the organization's nominating process is oriented toward identifying the person with the right qualities to lead the board as its chair (see Question 19).

- Keep the size of the board under control. Many organizations work well with a board of seven to fifteen members. They may have no executive committee and just a few standing committees.

- If the board has an executive committee, define its authority in the bylaws and use the committee creatively to help the full board and the chief executive function more effectively. An executive committee should never replace the full board even if it may be able to act on behalf of one under special circumstances (see Question 17).

- If the organization has paid staff members, don't allow the board chair to act as the chief executive (see Question 59).

- Clearly designate the chief executive as the sole agent of the board. In other words, all board business should flow through the chief executive, whether it comes from board to staff or from staff to board.

- Limit the number of standing committees—for example, the audit committee, the finance committee, and the governance committee might be the only ones listed in the bylaws (see Question 15).

- Use short-term committees and ad hoc task forces to address special needs that arise. Appoint the best people to these task forces, even if they are not board members, and issue a specific charge.

- When helpful, form an advisory council to provide specific expertise to the board (see Question 18).

- Limit board membership to volunteers. The one exception is the chief executive as an ex officio member (see Question 61).

SUGGESTED ACTION STEPS

1. Board chair, contract with an outside consultant. Ask each board member to write an unsigned memo to the consultant outlining likes and dislikes about the current board structure. Use the summary report prepared by the consultant as the starting point for a board discussion of how to increase effectiveness.

2. Board members, appoint a task force to review the structure of five organizations similar to yours and provide a report to the board.

Q A 15.

What types of board committees should we have?

Like most board members, you undoubtedly want to devote less time to attending meetings and engaging in busy work and more time to putting your expertise and experience to use on behalf of the organization. Being useful means serving on committees that truly do board-level work instead of standing (ongoing) committees that may have outlived their purpose.

Consider appointing these standing committees:

- *Audit committee*, to oversee the organization's regular outside financial audits. This committee's primary responsibility is to select and work with the independent, outside auditor who annually reviews the organization's financial systems and reports.

- *Finance committee*, to help the board fulfill its fiscal responsibilities. Members of this committee typically review budgets prepared by the staff, ensure that financial reports prepared by the staff are accurate and timely, make policy recommendations to the board, and provide other board members with explanations and insights into the organization's financial situation.

- *Governance committee*, to handle overall board development. Its responsibilities typically include determining the priorities for board composition, identifying and recruiting potential board candidates, organizing orientation for new board members, organizing ongoing education for the entire board, and overseeing board evaluation activities.

Beyond these three, other committees can come and go as organizational needs dictate. *Board-appointed committees* should deal with policies and strategies. *Organizational committees* should focus on issues or concerns related to specific programs or service delivery. Organizational committees, which do not necessarily need representation from the board, often are run by staff members.

Other committees commonly found in nonprofit organizations include the following:

- *Executive committee.* If your organization has or forms one, be perfectly clear about its role and what benefits it might bring to the board (see Question 17).

- *Investment committee.* If you have an investment portfolio, consider creating a separate investment committee to set the priorities and monitor the investment manager's performance.

- *Development (or advancement) committee.* By providing guidance, members of this committee support the staff's efforts to attract financial support through various initiatives and events. They have the responsibility of ensuring that all board members are involved in the organization's fundraising efforts (see Question 6).

- *Membership committee.* In particular, trade associations and professional societies may form a special committee to help recruit and retain dues-paying members and identify the best ways to serve them.

According to research conducted by BoardSource, just over half of the responding organizations (53 percent) have fewer than five standing committees. One in three (32 percent) has between five and ten committees. Most common are the executive committee (found in 80 percent of responding organizations), the governance committee (78 percent), and the finance committee (76 percent).

Resist the temptation to create a committee for every new initiative or emerging issue. Instead, appoint a *task force* to oversee a special project or assignment that has a set timeline (such as a capital campaign or bylaws review), then dissolve it upon completion of the project. Convening short-term task forces as the need arises not only makes board members feel needed but also restricts their time commitment. In addition, the concentrated focus ensures that the group is doing necessary and effective work.

The key is to keep the number of committees not only manageable but also appropriate to the organization's needs.

SUGGESTED ACTION STEPS

1. Board members, periodically review the board's policies and bylaws to ensure that the standing committees outlined within the policies are still necessary and relevant.

2. Board members, if you have several committees related to one program or project, combine them. One committee, with subcommittees or task groups, is enough.

16.

How can our committees be most effective?

Committees are simply one way a governing board organizes itself to be more efficient and effective. To ensure that you'll have a better idea of how effective your current committee structure is—or could be—answer the following questions.

- Do we want committees, or can the full board deal with all business itself?

- How does each standing committee's purpose relate to our mission and goals? Remember that the organization's needs will change periodically.

- What benefit does each committee provide to the board and to the entire organization? Insist that all committees focus on activities that help the full board do its work.

- Do any committees do duplicate work? They should supplement and build upon, not duplicate, work done by the staff or other committees. For instance, if you feel a need to form program committees, make sure they focus on evaluation.

- Do we need to amend our bylaws or policies to reflect our decisions about committees? The bylaws, for example, might simply authorize the board to "create such standing or other committees or task forces as the board may determine from time to time and describe in its standing policies." Then the standing rules would document the details of the various committees, including the function, size, membership, staffing, and appointment process for each one.

Selection of Members

Your organization's governance committee might be charged with matching individual board members to the committees' needs and with ensuring that each committee has the right mix of personalities. Often the board chair and the chief executive are best equipped to map out committee assignments and identify a potential chair. A good policy to include in bylaws might read, "The chair [or governance committee] shall appoint committee members and chairs, subject to the approval of the full board."

For a committee to be effective, its chair must be a good manager of people and process, someone who feels confident in guiding committee members to accomplish the task in a timely fashion. The job requires extra homework, regular communication with staff members and the board chair, and a willingness to resolve conflicts among committee members. It is not an honorary role.

The bylaws should allow a board to appoint some committee members from outside the board. This practice enables you to bring on expertise that the board itself may not have—an investment adviser for the finance committee, for example, if there is no separate investment committee. You will also be able to groom future board members and involve people who are willing to volunteer on a specific issue but are not yet ready to commit to the full role of a board member.

Because most board members are busy people, it's best to ask each to serve on only one standing committee as part of his or her board responsibilities. They might also be appointed to an ad hoc task force that focuses on a one-time assignment or project.

Appropriate Roles

No matter what its specific duty, a committee speaks *to* the board, not *for* the board. In other words, committees cannot think and act as mini-boards. Although a standing committee may draft changes to organizational policies and present them to the board for adoption, they do not have the jurisdiction to set board policy. Another appropriate role for a committee involves serving as a sounding board for senior staff members, providing advice, when asked, to the person responsible for managing the area of the committee's responsibility.

Advice to the staff, however, usually is offered when board members are wearing their volunteer hats (see Question 2), which applies to serving on committees. Consequently, staff members are free to solicit advice from many sources and other volunteers, not just from board committees.

The staff liaison still reports to the chief executive, not to the committee, and only helps the committee fulfill its assignment.

Some organizations that have few staff members require the chief executive to serve as the liaison to most committees. Larger organizations typically have an executive whose role matches the committee's area of responsibility and is asked by the chief executive to staff the committee. The board might set a policy that the chief executive will assign a staff member to work with each committee chair in preparing agenda material, maintaining good communications, and preparing minutes.

The specialized focus of committees enables board members to delve into specific areas and develop wise recommendations for board policy. In this way, committees usually add to a board member's enjoyment of board service.

SUGGESTED ACTION STEPS

1. Board members, clarify in your bylaws or policies why you have committees and which should be ongoing, standing committees. The board may decide some are no longer necessary.

2. Board members, consider how you might use temporary, or special, committees or task forces to focus on a project or topic that does not fit into the current committee structure.

3. Board members, review the charge issued by the board to each committee, to ensure that it is both specific and appropriate.

17.

Does our board need an executive committee?

Tradition should not dictate whether your organization has an executive committee—a subgroup of the board, typically composed of the board chair and several officers. Whether your board has always—or never—had one, the following principles apply to the role of an executive committee:

- It should not be a complete surrogate for the board itself.
- The full board should affirm the committee's decisions.

Unlike other standing committees, the executive committee speaks *to* the board as well as *for* the board. It speaks to the board whenever the board gives this committee responsibility over an aspect of governance, such as reviewing the bylaws, reexamining the mission statement, or evaluating the organization's goals. The committee would meet to deliberate on these issues and recommend changes to the board.

The executive committee speaks for the board when the board gives the committee authority to act on its behalf. Having this "back-up system" for the full board has several benefits—provided the committee does not overreach its authority. For international, national, or regional boards that meet only a few times a year, for example, an executive committee is an efficient mechanism for convening a smaller number of people to make timely board decisions. For large boards (more than thirty members), the executive committee is a more workable group for dealing with some routine issues. An organization in the midst of major restructuring or experiencing a crisis, for example, might require frequent board decisions on short notice, when it's not practical to convene the entire board. An executive committee can easily meet in person or via a telephone conference call.

Within a week or two, minutes of an executive committee meeting should be prepared and distributed to all board members. At its next meeting, the full board should confirm the committee's decisions; this clarifies the official record and ensures that the entire board is aware of the executive committee's actions.

Reflecting his or her status on the full board, the board chair almost always chairs the executive committee. Likewise, the chief executive serves on the executive committee in the same capacity as on the board. If the chief executive is an ex officio member of the board, then he or she should also be an ex officio member of the executive committee.

A Caution

The danger inherent in executive committees is that, over time, the full board may relax its sense of commitment and accountability and the executive committee may inadvertently take on responsibilities and decisions that belong to the full board. This may happen when a board chair and chief executive decide that full board meetings are too divisive, get bogged down in details, never finish the agenda, or suffer from lack of quorums. Instead of trying to fix the board problems, they divert decisions to the executive committee and marginalize the authority and commitment of many board members.

Some board members—whether or not they serve on the executive committee—may develop a we-they attitude. Board members who feel as if "insiders" are making all the key decisions may feel their commitment to the board waver if they believe they are simply rubber stamping the executive committee's decisions. Conversely, members of the executive committee may become so insular and focused on their activities that they inadvertently shut out other board members who would have valuable input. Either situation can lead to a drop in attendance at full board meetings and damage board unity.

If your board has not reached clear consensus on whether to have an executive committee, take an intermediate approach. Amend the bylaws to specify that the board may establish an executive committee to act on behalf of the board, when necessary, between regular board meetings.

When authorizing an executive committee, put reasonable limits on its authority. For example, state in the bylaws, "The executive committee may not amend the bylaws, hire or terminate the chief executive, elect or terminate board members, purchase or sell property, or dissolve the organization. Notices and minutes of executive committee meetings must be provided to all board members. All actions of the executive committee are subject to later review by the board."

SUGGESTED ACTION STEPS

1. Board members, in light of where the board and the organization are today, ask, Do we need an executive committee? If so, how should we limit its authority and how often should it meet?

2. Board members, evaluate the minutes of the past four or five board meetings to see which low-priority issues could have been delegated to an executive committee so the board itself could have focused on the major strategic issues.

3. Board members, if you have an executive committee, write a job description that clarifies its relationship to the full board.

18.

Should our board
have advisory councils?

Besides common administrative advisory committees to help staff members do their work more effectively, many boards of nonprofit organizations can benefit from the formation of an advisory council to provide advice and support. Perhaps a small group of financial experts could advise the board on its endowment investment policies, or the organization might create a council of board alumni to benefit from the continued engagement of its supporters. Some membership organizations appoint an editorial advisory group in the area of publications. Nonprofits undertaking capital campaigns often create a council with high-profile members to encourage contributions from others. Another possibility is to form a council of people who are knowledgeable about or use the organization's programs so they can help the board monitor results.

First, think through whether one or more advisory councils would help the organization achieve its mission. Even if it might never need to convene as a group, an advisory council can provide added credibility as well as access to special expertise. Its members bring new contacts and networks within the community, along with the possibility of financial contributions. A council may also serve as a training ground for new leaders. Often, council members develop so much knowledge of the organization and interest in its activities that they become prime candidates for future board service.

However, advisory councils require an investment of time and effort—usually by the chief executive, who often serves as the liaison. Some advisory council members may not be seen by all as a positive association for your organization or may try to compete with the board in wanting to make organizational decisions. You can minimize such risks by following these suggestions.

PART
2

- *Set guidelines for creating advisory councils.* Both the board and the staff should have the authority to create advisory groups—but one group or person should not impose an advisory mechanism on another. The board has the prerogative to set parameters for advisory groups, such as approving their budgets. The board itself may decide to name one or more formal advisory groups, particularly to help them link to a larger, more diverse constituency.

- *Choose an appropriate name.* Avoid names that use the word *board*, which can lead constituents to confuse advisory groups with the governing board. The name instead might reflect the purpose of the group or emphasize the level of expertise and leadership qualities of its members.

- *Describe the group's role.* Create a written description of each advisory council's purposes and accountability. Clarify that the group does not make final decisions for the organization; by definition, it has an advisory role. Some groups never meet as a whole but are willing to be called upon individually or in small groups for specific purposes at different times. Others need to convene regularly to discuss and draft their recommendations.

- *Establish terms of service.* People also like to know what they are getting into when they agree to volunteer commitments, so consider renewable terms. Thank everyone at the end of the term, and invite some to continue.

- *Provide for formal leadership.* Volunteers often respond better when one of their own chairs an advisory council. This additional leadership role is often substantively and politically helpful to the board chair or the chief executive.

- *Plan for staff assistance.* Like board committees, advisory councils often need a staff liaison. The chief executive should select this person or fill the role personally.

- *Budget for any expenses.* If the council convenes in person, the organization should be prepared to pay out-of-pocket expenses for the council members who attend. This can be a sizable budget item. (*Note:* If the organization does not provide reimbursement, all nonreimbursed expenses related to volunteer service for a 501(c)(3) are tax deductible.)

- *Provide appropriate publicity.* Many advisory councils are designed to give constituents, current and potential donors, foundations, and other organizations more confidence in the organization. Giving public recognition to these people and their efforts is certainly acceptable, but guard against providing more publicity than is warranted.

Whatever their area of expertise, advisory councils work best when the board is clear about the councils' specific roles and responsibilities from the start. Whatever the advisory council's charge, its members need to understand the limits of their authority; specifically, they can suggest actions for the board to take, but the board is under no obligation to implement their recommendations.

SUGGESTED ACTION STEPS

1. Board members, brainstorm for ten minutes about areas within the organization—board or staff—where outside advice might be used effectively.

2. Chief executive, interview the chief executives of five organizations that have advisory councils. Summarize their experiences for other board members to discuss.

3. Board members, terminate an advisory council that no longer serves a purpose.

Q A

19.

What is the role
of the board chair?

Regardless of how much leadership experience or professional expertise one has, serving as the board chair is unlike any other job. Even veteran leaders, who have served as the board chair of more than one organization, often comment on how different each position is because of the different mission, objectives, strategies, and personalities involved.

No doubt about it, the board chair has a demanding and multifaceted job that goes far beyond banging the gavel to signal the start and the end of each board meeting. In addition to all the primary responsibilities of being a board member (see Question 1), the board chair also has specific responsibilities related to leading the group that provide organizational oversight. These additional duties include the following.

Preside at board meetings. Finding a chair with the ability to manage group process should be an important consideration in officer elections, and should take precedence over selecting a chair who is personally popular, has a close relationship with the chief executive, has been on the board the longest, or has made a sizable financial contribution. At times in the boardroom, the board chair will need to initiate or facilitate conversation, motivate board members to engage more deeply with the organization, bring calm to a tense situation, and exert control over a discussion that has ranged far afield. Doing so requires an awareness of group dynamics and a specific skills set—all of which can be learned, provided the board chair has the willingness.

PART 2

Coauthor board agendas. Well in advance of a meeting, the board chair and chief executive should discuss what should be on the agenda, how much time to give to key items, whether guests should be invited to make presentations, how long staff reports should take (most can be sent out in advance), and whether to have an executive session without staff members present.

Appoint and assist committees. Whether the bylaws give appointment authority to the full board or to the chair, the board chair should have considerable influence in committee assignments. This responsibility requires knowing the interests and availability of all board members. It also calls for fairness and balance in matching personalities to group tasks. Consultation is always required, but the board chair is the one who understands the strengths and weaknesses of the other board members and the chief executive. He or she is most aware of the broad picture.

Many bylaws make the board chair an ex officio member of all committees. *Ex officio* simply means "by reason of the office"—in other words, board chairs are not elected or named to the committees but serve as committee members because of the position they hold within the greater organization. Of course, few board chairs have the time—or the need—to attend many committee meetings. This is understandable, but board chairs should invest orientation time up front with at least the committee chair, if not with each committee. Everyone benefits from knowing the board chair's expectations, the time frame for decisions, and the committee's authority to call on staff for help.

Appoint a search committee. One special responsibility of the board chair is to appoint and issue the charge to a search committee for a new chief executive. Although not all chairs will have to face this difficult task, they should understand this key role if the need arises (see Question 70).

Manage group development. Some decisions—such as board size, term of service, and committee structure—are made by the full board and codified in the bylaws or policies. But the board chair often initiates recommendations to change board policy. And other group process decisions are often left to the chair's discretion, such as when to call special meetings, when to refer an issue to a committee, or how to handle an inactive board member.

Maintain organizational integrity. The board chair has a legal mandate from the state in which the organization is founded to assume overall responsibility for the board and to ensure that the organization's mission is respected. An arm's-length relationship to daily operations is necessary to fulfill this role objectively as the organization's legal and moral authority. Most organizations can survive temporary crises; few can survive the loss of public trust. The board chair's internal watch is critical because few board members take the time, or exercise the courage, to tackle issues such as executive compensation, allowable expenses, and truthfulness in fundraising appeals.

Forge a link with the major stakeholders. One task of a board member is to stay in touch with the organization's major constituencies. Although the staff does this constantly, at times the board chair is the most appropriate person to represent the organization at a key meeting, appear on a radio or television talk show, write a magazine column, serve as the organization's spokesperson, preside at a membership forum, make a presentation at a community event, or thank major donors (see Question 10). Depending on the situation, the best results are achieved when the board chair and chief executive do something together.

Support the chief executive. The board chair needs to keep an ear to the ground, sound out individual board members, and then gently encourage the chief executive in the direction of positive board relationships. Chief executives need encouragement as well as feedback on their performance. They appreciate affirmation from the board chair, along with kind notes, quick calls to check in, or offers to do something together. These seemingly small actions build the foundation of a relationship that will withstand inevitable times of tension (see Question 20).

PART
2

Be clear on the chair's and chief executive's roles and responsibilities. The board chair should revisit with the chief executive all of their respective roles and responsibilities to clarify who handles what (see Question 59). There's little, if anything, for an organization to gain when its two most prominent representatives jockey for public recognition or engage in a tug-of-war contest on an issue. When the board chair and the chief executive agree to do whatever is necessary to make the other successful, the success of the board and the organization will follow.

SUGGESTED ACTION STEPS

1. Board chair and chief executive, schedule a lunch to discuss the responsibilities for the chair. Present to the board for approval any necessary changes in the bylaws or standing policies, so that everyone is making the same assumptions and holding the chair to the same expectations.

2. Board chair, invite the board chairs of five or six other nonprofit organizations in the community to attend an informal get-together. "Talking shop" offers one means of deepening knowledge and developing new skills.

20.

What is the ideal relationship between the board chair and the chief executive?

Several situations can hamper a board chair's effectiveness. For instance, some board members may treat the chair as if he or she is the chief executive. They ask operational questions and set expectations that are more appropriate for the staff leader of the organization. This is more likely to occur in organizations that get started without a full-time paid staff.

In those cases, the board chair often plays the dual role of running board meetings and serving as the senior implementer of policy. Habits develop. Then, when a paid chief executive is hired, people may continue looking to the board chair for day-to-day leadership. The chief executive is relegated to the role of chief operating officer or even office manager. To avoid this, roles must be clearly delineated and the bylaws changed to reflect the chief executive's responsibilities as staff leader (see Question 59).

Another problem arises when a chief executive, particularly one who was a founder of the organization, views the board chair as a competitor or a threat. The chief executive may try to keep the board chair in the dark—never discussing meeting agendas, board development, committee structure, or other matters—except to preside over formal business meetings.

Unfortunately, some of these strong founder-chief executives write the script (often in the bylaws) that they will function as both chief executive and board chair.

These situations simply don't work. A nonprofit organization needs both a volunteer board chair and a paid chief executive. Following are some reasons why:

- A board benefits from the insights and perspectives of both leaders who are responsible for a different set of functions within the organization.

- Accountability helps maintain the credibility of a nonprofit organization; a chief executive needs to be accountable to the board. If he or she also serves as board chair, an obvious conflict of interest exists.

- Managing the organization is a full-time job. Board members, including chairs, generally have their own professional lives that require their attention and primary time commitment.

- Boards need to feel important, needed, and strategically significant to organizational success. This happens more readily when one of their own is in a leadership role.

It Takes Two

Like a marriage or a business partnership, the chief executive–board chair relationship brings together two people with distinct personalities, experiences, preferences, perspectives, operating styles, and decision-making modes. Furthermore, both are proven leaders, meaning each also has healthy doses of self-confidence, vision, energy, and innovative ideas. Put them together, and you're bound to have disagreements.

How those disagreements play out within the organization and are ultimately resolved will determine the effectiveness of the board chair's term in office. Allowing tensions to build and spill over into relationships with other board and staff members can create divided loyalties. Everyone devotes his or her time to rehashing or second guessing what one of the leaders said or did instead of focusing on the business at hand.

In contrast, chief executives and board chairs who acknowledge that they are equal partners and make a commitment to a relationship of mutual trust can keep the organization moving ahead. The board chair must trust his or her own abilities to fulfill the job's many responsibilities and trust the chief executive to do the same, and vice versa.

Following are suggestions for the board chair to arrive at that level of trust.

Review your respective roles and responsibilities. Knowing your boundaries, as prescribed by your respective job descriptions, will make you less likely to overstep them.

Of course, every board and staff member can probably recite the mantra: the board handles strategy, while the staff handles operations. But what does that mean? Simply put, the board is responsible for the ends and the staff is responsible for the means. To use a nautical analogy, the board determines where the organization needs to head, charts the appropriate course, and checks progress along the way. The staff members, with the chief executive as their captain, move the organization toward its destination, taking care to avoid rough waters.

Because it is responsible for governance—including setting policies and goals, keeping the organization true to its mission, and monitoring performance—the board does not become involved in day-to-day operations. As board chair, the last thing on your mind should be hiring or firing staff members (with the exception of the chief executive), doling out assignments to employees, or deciding which phone system the organization should purchase.

Conversely, the chief executive concentrates on implementing board decisions, not publicly disagreeing with board members or ignoring outright the decisions that he or she doesn't personally approve. Being an integral part of the strategies and goals discussions, the chief executive naturally will go with the flow and restructure the staff or take on new tasks accordingly. For instance, a staff structured to support growth in fundraising will look different from one with an intense focus on program delivery.

Revisit the organization. No matter how long you have been involved in the organization or have served on its board, take the time to reread key documents: bylaws, articles of incorporation, board policies, and the strategic plan. Also look over the previous year's financial statements, annual report, and audit. You've undoubtedly seen all of these before, but not necessarily through the eyes of the board chair. Brush up on parliamentary procedure as well so that you feel comfortable running meetings even if strict formality is not the style of your board.

Review the strategic plan. What are the strategic priorities for the year? If the board and staff have agreed on what the organization will do (annual operating objectives) and how much it will spend (annual operating budget), then both the chief executive and the board chair will have their work cut out for them. There won't be time (or money) for either to launch a new initiative merely on a whim.

Focusing on the strategic plan underscores the common ground on which both the staff and the board operate. Everyone is working toward the same goal: the organization's success.

Set personal goals. Every board chair wants to be remembered for accomplishments, not failures. But leaving your indelible mark on the organization should not come at the expense of its overall objectives. More than one organization has lost ground in a fundraising campaign or failed to develop a key initiative because the board chair had a pet project that siphoned off valuable financial and staff resources. And more often than not, those projects become distant memories just a few years later.

To leave a lasting legacy, link your personal goals to the organization's overall strategic plan. Zero in on the one or two areas where you believe you can be most effective, then discuss with the chief executive what you'd like to accomplish.

Spend time on the other's turf. Set aside a day to spend at the organization's headquarters—not just sitting in the chief executive's office but meeting with employees and getting a feel for how the organization operates. In turn, familiarize the chief executive with your professional environment so he or she can better understand the daily pressures you face in addition to your board responsibilities. The insights gained can help forge a stronger partnership.

Set up a communication schedule with the chief executive. After reviewing your individual roles, responsibilities, and commitments, discuss the best way to stay in touch. For example, you might set aside a certain time on the same day each week to talk by phone. Or perhaps you'd prefer to exchange regular e-mail updates.

In those exchanges, communicate what you are doing on behalf of the organization; whom you have talked to about what; and what upcoming commitments are on your calendar, such as speaking engagements, meeting with other nonprofits, or attending orientation for board nominees.

Keep your communications open and honest. If you don't want to be bothered by ten e-mails or five phone calls from the chief executive every day, say so, and offer an alternative means of communication. If you'd rather not do a lot of public speaking or testify before elected officials, share that feeling so that someone else can cover for you. If you think board meetings take too long, consult with the chief executive on how you can change the status quo.

When it comes to management of the organization, however, your preferred style or way of doing business doesn't matter. The day-to-day operations remain the chief executive's responsibility.

Serve as a role model. Both board and staff members will take their cues from their respective leader. If the board chair badmouths the chief executive or circumvents his or her authority, for example, the whole environment will be tense and antagonistic. But a collegial culture prevails in organizations in which the board chair and chief executive work as a team and support and applaud one another's efforts and accomplishments.

As the board chair, you're also a role model within the community. How you speak about the chief executive reflects on the organization itself and draws the attention of donors, dues-paying members, reporters, and the general public.

In your quest to be an effective leader, just remember that you're not alone. The chief executive reports to the board, not just to you; the board, not you on your own, establishes policies, sets strategic direction, monitors organizational performance, and evaluates its own effectiveness (see Question 1).

PART
2

SUGGESTED ACTION STEPS

1. Board chair and chief executive, attend a partnership-building seminar or conference and discuss specific ways to work more effectively together.

2. Board members, incorporate a discussion of the board–staff partnership into orientation for new board members; use the board chair–chief executive relationship as an example of how the board's responsibility (determining the ends or results) differs from the staff's responsibility (developing the means within board parameters).

21.

What board officers
should we have?

Board officers are the leaders of the board. They provide conceptual leadership and model the board's working culture—the tone and approach for its interactions. From a practical standpoint, officers coordinate board activities and are responsible for special assignments. If a nonprofit organization has an executive committee, it is typically composed of the board officers and the chief executive (see Question 17).

At a minimum, as defined by state laws, most boards have the following officers:

Chair. On most boards, this position requires the greatest time commitment. The chair manages the board and serves as the primary liaison between the board and the chief executive (see Questions 19 and 20).

Vice chair. This position provides additional leadership, substituting for the chair when that person is not available or leaves the position before the end of his or her term. Often, a board calls upon the vice chair to lead special projects, such as heading the governance committee or facilitating the chief executive's annual review. Some boards elect more than one vice chair, with each one overseeing a particular project.

Treasurer. The person elected to this position assumes the primary volunteer role in the organization's financial oversight. The treasurer oversees financial operations, ensuring that incoming revenues and outgoing payments are handled and recorded appropriately. In a smaller organization, the treasurer may have the hands-on responsibility for writing checks, recording payments, and preparing financial reports. In a larger organization, those duties are typically handled by the chief financial officer, controller, or accountant. Under all circumstances, some segregation of duties is necessary.

Some boards also elect the following officers.

Secretary. This position has the responsibility for ensuring that board-related documents—primarily minutes of board meetings—are accurate and prepared in a timely manner. In a smaller organization, the secretary may have the responsibility for taking and distributing the minutes; in a larger organization, he or she will review the minutes prepared by staff members before they are distributed to the board for approval. The secretary may also take on related duties delegated by the board, such as overseeing the implementation of a records-management system for the board.

Some organizations combine the duties of secretary and treasurer into one position, especially when the staff essentially carries out the tasks specific to these positions. In fact, it's not unusual for staff members to actually do the work related to the position of board secretary and, to some extent, treasurer. The appropriate board officer then has the responsibility of reviewing and approving the minutes or financial reports. Once approved, the documents themselves are usually kept in the organization's headquarters.

Chair-elect. To ensure leadership continuity—and to acclimate the incoming chair to the responsibilities ahead—some nonprofit organizations designate a chair-elect. This person has already been designated as the successor to the current board chair, on the basis of the board's policies and election processes (see Question 22). He or she is often given specific tasks, such as chairing the strategic planning task force, and may have the responsibility of presiding at a board meeting in the chair's absence.

The bylaws should spell out the general responsibilities of the organization's officers. In addition, it's helpful to develop a detailed job description for each officer position, to clarify expectations. As the organization matures, these responsibilities may change, so be sure to schedule a periodic review of the bylaws and update them when necessary.

SUGGESTED ACTION STEPS

1. Board members, benchmark other nonprofit organizations to ascertain how they define and allocate responsibilities among the board officers.

2. Board members, consider electing an assistant secretary and assistant treasurer from the staff or allow the chief executive to designate a staff member to handle the tasks—not the monitoring—that the bylaws prescribe for the secretary and treasurer.

22.

How should we select our board officers?

There are three common ways to elect officers. The board should discuss these options and decide what is best for the organization in light of its culture and personality.

Adoption of an uncontested slate. The first—and preferred—method is by adopting an uncontested slate. The governance committee looks at all the possibilities, talks informally with board members and potential candidates, and presents a slate of officers to the full board. If the process has been open and careful, the slate is adopted with no nominations from the floor.

When the committee presents two or more candidates for each position, each board member has a choice to make. But this approach tends to create "losers" and affect board morale. It's preferable to have a strong governance committee that, after communicating among board members and candidates, presents a single candidate who has everyone's support.

Selection by a parent organization or outside appointing authority.
The same entity probably would appoint or elect all board members, simply designating some as officers. The drawback to this method is that the appointing authorities may not actually see how these officers perform. Internal politics—such as who has served the longest, who has the most free time, who is the biggest donor, or who the chief executive wants on the executive committee—may also unduly influence the selection.

Open election. For each officer position, an envelope is passed around the table. Each board member writes a name on an index card and inserts it into the envelope. Someone tallies and announces the vote. If no one receives a majority, the envelope is passed around again, until one person receives a majority of the board's votes. The process is repeated until all officers are elected.

This process gives the elected officer a sense of confidence and accountability to do the job well because he or she has the trust of every board member. It might be the preferred method if the board feels that a group of insiders controls elections. But it also has limitations. For instance, a candidate may stay in the race simply because he or she feels flattered to have been considered. The process also makes it difficult for the chief executive to express concerns about the candidates. Most important, it may not produce officers who are well-matched to their jobs.

Match to the Job

Officer elections should not be popularity contests. The skills, experience, and temperament of a person top the list of the most important qualifications for an officer's position. The board's goal should be to

- Elect people whose strengths fit the task.
- Elect each officer, after the governance committee has evaluated current officers. Officers who have received positive evaluations and are willing to continue can be reelected.

- Give others the opportunity to serve in leadership positions by limiting how many years or terms an officer can serve (perhaps a maximum of five to six years).

Some boards automatically promote the vice chair to chair when the latter's term ends. This system ensures that incoming chairs are more experienced in board leadership, but it can be difficult for a vice chair to plan that far ahead. It's better to wait until the time comes, and nominate the candidate who is best prepared to serve as chair.

PART
2

SUGGESTED ACTION STEPS

1. Board chair, ask the governance committee or a small group of experienced board members to review the way officers are elected and evaluated and recommend changes.

2. Board members, review the bylaws to ensure that they clearly explain how the organization can elect its officers and how long they can remain in those positions.

PART THREE

Selection and Development of Board Members

When board members were surveyed by BoardSource, the vast majority (93 percent) said that the most important consideration when deciding whether to join a board was achieving a match between the organization's mission and their personal interests. That's a powerful connection to keep in mind during the ongoing search for new board members who will bring leadership, organizational planning, and other invaluable skills to the board.

In many nonprofits, the governance committee takes the lead in cultivating potential board members. But it can't do this important job alone. Involving the full board in identifying future leaders can lead to better governance. Cultivating, recruiting, and selecting board members requires deep thinking about the board's needs, which often stimulates the board to deal with important issues it might have otherwise overlooked. And once people have become board members, ongoing education about their roles and responsibilities will strengthen the connection that brought them to your organization's attention in the first place.

23.

How can we recruit active, involved board members?

A good response to this question is, "How would *you* like to be recruited?"

Perhaps you came to service on a board without much knowledge, much commitment, or much expectation. You might have felt confused about your role, uninformed about the decisions you were asked to make, or superfluous to the board's way of doing business. That's a recipe for inactive board members.

The seriousness with which a board member is recruited and selected is directly proportional to the seriousness with which that board member fulfills his or her role. So if you want to recruit people who are serious about governing the organization, you must take recruitment seriously. Following are the steps to take.

Define the board member's job. Develop a one- to two-page job description that suits the organization at this point in its lifecycle. Outline the basic responsibilities of each board member, as well as the expectations related to each of the three hats (governance, implementation, and volunteer) a board member wears (see Questions 1 and 2).

For instance, in addition to providing direction and monitoring activities, is a board member expected to give much time as a volunteer with the organization? Do you expect, as you should, that every board member will make a financial contribution each year? On how many committees is a board member expected to serve? How will a board member's performance be evaluated?

Agree on the profile of the future board. The board should describe what the "dream team" it envisions will look like in a few years. For example, describe minimums, maximums, or percentages for whatever characteristics are important for your organization. These could include age, gender, and minority representation, as well as lay versus professional, rural versus urban, and other demographic variables (see Question 26). The profile should be unique to your organization's current stage of development. Exhibit 23.1 can be used or adapted to create profiles of current and prospective members.

EXHIBIT 23.1. Board Member Profile.

Desired Characteristics	Current Members			Prospective Members		
All Members Should Have These Characteristics	1	2	3	1	2	3
Demonstrated interest before nomination						
Was a donor of record in previous year						
Has some experience in our area of service						
Board service is supported by his or her family						
Is able to attend meetings; is able to give eight to ten days a year						
Is known as good group decision maker						
Other:						

EXHIBIT 23.1. Board Member Profile, Cont'd.

Desired Characteristics	Current Members			Prospective Members		
Each Member Should Have One or More of These Characteristics	*1*	*2*	*3*	*1*	*2*	*3*
Is a recognized community leader						
Has prior experience on nonprofit boards						
Has knowledge of nonprofit law						
Has knowledge of nonprofit fundraising						
Has specialized knowledge of one mission or program area						
Helps balance the board in terms of gender						
Helps balance the board in terms of age						
Helps balance the board in terms of ethnicity						
Helps balance the board in terms of skills and expertise						
Has experience in marketing our services						
Is a good mediator of group disagreements						
Has knowledge of land use and facilities management						
Has experience in dealing with local government						
Has a network of donor prospects						
Has or had leadership in another organization important to us						
Other:						
Other:						

PART
3

Develop qualifications for serving. After the board member profile has been created by the governance committee and approved by
the entire board, use it to identify current or projected gaps in the
desired experience and qualifications of board members. If, for example, a member with an expertise in fundraising will be rotating
off the board in a year, at least one new member should have that
same expertise. Doing this enables the organization to build a team
of people who bring a balanced array of specialized talents and skills
to the collective effort.

Adopt a plan to identify and nurture prospects. Using your expectations and needed qualifications as a guide, come up with a list of
the people who might be best for the board at this time. All board
members, the chief executive, and even senior staff members should
be encouraged to participate in this ongoing process of identifying
future leaders, either by suggesting names themselves or contacting
major donors, friends in other nonprofits, or neighbors for possible
names.

Once you have a list of people who meet most qualifications,
find meaningful ways to involve them as volunteers before asking
them to join the board. They might serve on a task force or committee, host an event, or contribute their expertise to a special
project. If a person is responsive at this level, he or she is more likely
to participate at the board level as well.

Gradually expand the prospective board member's involvement
in the organization. Eventually, if he or she is not yet a donor, ask for
a contribution. If you ask more than once but still get no response,
beware. The person is probably not yet ready for board membership.

Have a rigorous nomination process. The governance committee
is now ready to consider a slate of known talent to fill the most critical needs on the board. Look at balance. Determine who could be
groomed for a key leadership role down the road, knowing who is
likely to leave the board.

Assign someone to meet personally with each highly rated prospect. The board contact can invite the prospect to read the job description, review organizational documents (such as the bylaws or a brief history), and decide whether to be considered for board service.

When a prospect shows interest, provide a thorough explanation of what board service entails, so that there are no surprises later (see Question 27). In turn, find out the person's own motivations for serving by asking, "What three or four things would you hope to gain personally from serving on our board?" Whether the person hopes to develop new skills, find new friends, or achieve a higher visibility within the community, make sure those personal goals and expectations are reasonable and complement the organization's mission and values.

PART
3

You might want to conduct a reference check at this stage in the nominating process. Few organizations hire a staff member without consulting references, and board members have an equally important role within the organization.

Take board election and new member orientation seriously. Make the actual election and welcoming event memorable for new board members. These first impressions will last a long time.

SUGGESTED ACTION STEPS

1. Board members, list your reasons for serving on the board. Do you have realistic expectations that match the mission of the organization and the roles and responsibilities of board members?

2. Board members, reflect on how you were recruited for board service and how that experience could be improved.

24.

What is the chief executive's role in board recruitment?

More than a few nonprofit board members, particularly business owners, think the board should be made up only of people the chief executive chooses. That's the way many small businesses work. But the board must own the responsibility to improve its own strength and effectiveness, which includes taking the lead in recruiting new members.

In fact, recruitment requires a collaborative effort of the board and the chief executive, with the board leading the process. When board members are actively involved in recruitment, they become more committed to helping their new colleagues succeed at board service. In addition, the chief executive will be more accountable for his or her actions when reporting to a board that includes people other than personal friends. It is a clear conflict of interest for a chief executive to handpick the board members who ultimately assess his or her performance and determine his or her compensation.

Chief executives should certainly be involved in the process of selecting board members, but they should not vote on who is elected. Specifically, it is entirely appropriate for the chief executive to

- Help the board draft appropriate criteria for board membership
- Be engaged in identifying candidates along with other staff and board members
- Nurture the interest of potential board members
- Consult with the board during the recruitment process, expressing concerns about candidates when appropriate
- Brief candidates on the organization and the nonprofit sector in general
- Follow up the board's election with a welcome call or letter and an orientation program

SUGGESTED ACTION STEPS

1. Board members, identify ways in which the board selection process can be a balanced partnership between the board and the chief executive.

2. Board members, interview the three newest members of the board to learn their opinions about the process and their suggestions for improvement.

25.

PART
3

How can a membership organization build an effective board?

Although the same principles of nonprofit governance apply to most boards, not all boards are alike. In fact, membership-based organizations typically select their board members in a way significantly different from other nonprofits.

In a membership organization, the members typically elect the board. This approach reflects the democratic process by which people are elected to school boards, state legislatures, the U.S. Congress, and the like. The underlying assumption is that people who have an interest in, and may be affected by, a group of decision makers should have the right to select those decision makers.

Many organizations with elected boards hold an election at the annual meeting of hundreds, even thousands, of members. A governance committee has developed a slate of people it believes will bring balance and expertise to the board. The process comes close to being a self-perpetuating board, but the larger membership still has the right to object to the slate and, although it's difficult, promote someone other than those on the governance committee's ballot.

Other organizations, at intervals specified in their bylaws, send a ballot and short biographies of the board candidates to all members. The ballot may be uncontested (having the same number of candidates as open positions) or contested (having more candidates than open positions). When contested, elections place some important volunteers in the position of being declared "losers" by their peers.

No matter how they are selected, elected boards always have the potential for being seen as a popularity contest, resulting in a board that lacks diversity and has less mutual accountability. To develop an effective elected board, a membership organization should do the following:

PART
3

- *Avoid setting strict representational quotas or using the board election to repay political favors.* Board members must see the organization as an entity, not as an agent for their particular constituents. The needs of the national organization must always take precedence over the needs of a particular chapter or group represented by a board member. Elected board members must leave their personal and professional agendas at the boardroom door.

- *Cast a wide net when seeking nominees.* The governance committee must take its job seriously, conducting an aggressive and open search throughout the organization for committed and qualified potential board members. It must understand the qualities of a good board member and be able to assess the characteristics required at a particular moment to maximize the effectiveness of the board's composition. Leadership succession planning is important, too, to ensure a pool of board candidates.

- *Present an uncontested slate to the membership.* If the governance committee does its homework thoroughly, involving the membership in the recruitment and cultivation process, it is able to narrow the slate of candidates to the best people for the job. Members can still make write-in nominations or nominations from the floor.

SUGGESTED ACTION STEPS

1. Board chair, schedule a board discussion and critique of the nomination and selection process.

2. Board chair, if even a few board members raise the need for change, appoint a task force to study and report on how other membership organizations approach this process.

Q A **26.**

How can our board become more diverse?

Boards that become too insular, either by electing the same people to leadership positions or by selecting new members in their same mold, can easily miss opportunities to strengthen the organization by introducing fresh perspectives and diverse voices. In addition, donors and the community at large will look at your board as a reflection of the entire organization. If they perceive that you are stuck in a rut or out of touch with what's happening in the wider world, they are more likely to lend their support elsewhere.

Diversity encompasses many elements: age, gender, ethnicity, geographic location, occupation, professional affiliation, skills set, and so forth. For a suburban-based nonprofit, for instance, diversity might mean board members from urban or rural areas. A board governing a nonprofit dedicated to young women's issues might seek to diversify by recruiting men and older women.

Reducing a board's homogeneity opens it to a variety of viewpoints and avenues of action. People from different backgrounds, who have had different experiences, will add a richness to the board's discussions, often raising points that other members would never have thought about. Of course, once a board has spoken with one voice on policy, those holding contrary opinions must be loyal to the majority.

One caution: a board should beware of tokenism—having, for example, "the young member" or "the Asian member" or "the member from the inner city." This type of approach does not reflect a serious attempt to diversify the board's composition and does a disservice to the people who were recruited to bring a fresh, personal perspective to board discussions and decisions. It is unfair and dangerous to expect one person to be the "representative" of a specific population. No one person can—or should—reflect the viewpoints of an entire group.

To encourage more diversity within its ranks, a board should

- Emphasize to the governance committee the importance of finding candidates who would bring a broader variety of experience and views to the board. They may be found among constituent groups, on boards of other organizations, or within subgroups of the membership or donor base.

- Provide the governance committee with the names of people you believe would bring needed expertise or diversity (gender, age, ethnic, or geographic) to the board.

- Actively solicit different points of view during board discussions, led by a chair who welcomes a broad spectrum of ideas and perspectives. No one should feel penalized for voicing what might be an unpopular view.

- To build more diverse networks and relationships that could yield future board members, invite nonboard members to sit on advisory councils or certain board committees.

- Hold joint meetings with leaders from groups that have traditionally been underrepresented on the board.

SUGGESTED ACTION STEPS

1. Board members, have an open discussion about how well the board reflects the diversity of its constituencies.

2. Board members, develop a list of desired qualifications for board membership, including the need for people of different ages, genders, religious beliefs, races, professional experiences, and so forth (see Question 23).

3. Board members, strategize about how best to identify and recruit people who will bring new perspectives to the governance process.

PART
3

27.

PART
3

What does a prospective board member need to know?

Have you ever received a call like this? "We voted last night to elect you to our board. Will you accept?" The caller often goes on to say, "This won't take a lot of your time. It's just a bunch of good people who enjoy being together."

Board service involves much more than that. The board has legal and moral responsibility for the organization (see Question 7). A governing board role should not be viewed as honorary or advisory or "just helping out my friend, the chief executive." Board membership should be a serious decision. Before agreeing to serve on a board, ask the following ten questions, at a minimum.

What is the mission of the organization? The mission should drive the whole organization. It should be clear and in writing. Policies and actions flowing from that mission should be evident. Can you support it? It is best if the organization's mission actually touches one of your personal passions. Can you give your best to ensure the mission's success? Halfhearted support does not help an organization.

According to BoardSource research, one in four board members (23 percent) said their main reason for joining a board was because of an invitation from a friend or colleague. But a much greater percentage (54 percent) said they joined because of their commitment to the organization's cause.

Who are the leaders of the organization? Do you know the organization leaders? Do you respect their reputations? As a new board member, you will discover that a strong board chair, or more typically the chief executive, often has enormous influence over board decisions. If you do not already know these people, find out more about them. If you do not respect the board chair and chief executive, service on the board will be difficult.

What is the financial condition of the organization? It's not unusual for a nonprofit board to struggle with finances. Ask for a copy of the most recent external audit and the current year's budget, plus the revenue and expenditure statement, cash flow budget, and balance sheet. Although you should contribute to the financial stability of any organization on whose board you serve, you need to join a board with your eyes wide open. Service on a board for which financial problems consume every meeting is not very fulfilling.

What is the board member's job description? Without a common understanding of what their roles are, board members can waste time and effort and become frustrated because of differing assumptions about what they should be doing. Probe to find out whether the current board agrees about its collective role and the role of individual board members.

How long is my term? Most boards elect members for terms of two or three years. Some, to encourage rotation and invite new perspectives, limit the number of consecutive terms. Find out if you are being considered for a full term or will be completing another board member's unexpired term. Ask whether reelection at the end of the

PART
3

stated term is essentially automatic and whether you will have the option to politely decline reelection when your term ends.

How much of my time will be required in a normal year? Most boards require the equivalent of a minimum of five to eight days per year. Many board members give much more. The expected time commitment includes preparation for board and committee meetings, the meetings themselves, travel, assignments, and special projects. Boards that meet outside your city may meet less often, but the travel time will increase, as will the likelihood that some board members may need to take time off of work to attend meetings. Decide whether you can commit to the time required.

How many meetings will I be expected to attend, and when are they? Meetings may take up less time than other responsibilities, but you may have standing commitments that conflict with an already-determined schedule of board meetings. Or if the board always meets on Saturdays, you may be unwilling to take that additional time away from your personal life. Committee meeting dates usually are flexible and are not set far in advance, whereas board meeting dates are often scheduled up to a year in advance. Also consider the major events the organization sponsors and which ones board members are expected to attend.

A related question is, "Do I enjoy group meetings?" Many people agree to serve on a board out of some charitable motivation, only later to acknowledge, "I hate sitting in meetings." But realize that boards fulfill their ultimate governance duties through deliberation and voting in a duly called meeting. Mere attendance is not enough. Participation is essential.

Who pays for my expenses as a board member? If no out-of-town travel is required, expenses for board service can be minimal. But they can be considerable if you have to fly to a few meetings, drive long distances, or stay in a hotel. Meals, long-distance calls, and other miscellaneous items contribute to the expense.

Many organizations assume that all board members are willing and able to be responsible for their own expenses, in addition to providing volunteer service. Clarify the board's expectations and be willing to accept them.

Are all board members expected to be donors? Every board member should support the organization he or she serves, no matter how large or small the financial contribution. But some boards depend on their members so much financially that you would not be elected unless you were viewed as a potential major donor. Just be clear about the extent of the expectation before agreeing to join the board.

In addition to being donors, most board members are expected to open doors to friends and acquaintances who might be contributors. Are you willing to do this?

What are my motivations for serving as a board member? Once you've gathered all this information, your own motivations will begin to emerge. By now you know it will take more time and money than you might have expected. You will be aware of some of the problems the organization faces. It looks like board service entails more than just the honor of being asked.

In the final analysis, you should not agree to serve out of a sense of obligation or guilt or to look good among your friends. Instead, consider the invitation to serve as an opportunity for personal reflection. Ask yourself, "How will service to this organization help me grow and allow me to contribute what I do best?" For board service to be a priority in your life, you need to consider the potential for personal enrichment.

If you are currently a board member, make sure you have the answers to these questions and touch on all of them when talking with prospective members. Tell as much about the organization as you can to someone being considered for the board.

PART
3

Exit Interviews

You can learn a lot about recruiting new board members from those who have completed their terms or resigned. The governance committee can conduct an exit interview with departing board members and gain insights by asking such questions as

- How much did the board focus its energies on fulfilling the organization's mission?
- How well were your expertise and abilities used during your term in office?
- Do you believe the expectations outlined before you became a board member matched the reality of the position?
- How do you feel you have contributed to the board's work? To the organization as a whole?
- Did you have any disappointments in relation to your role as a board member?
- Do you believe you received all the training you needed to serve effectively on the board? If not, what would have benefited you the most?
- In your view, what strategic priorities should the organization concentrate on during the next few years?
- In your view, what skills and competencies does the board need to cultivate among board members to meet the challenges ahead?

SUGGESTED ACTION STEPS

1. Prospective board members, ask to meet with the chief executive alone so you can ask probing questions about the organization and about his or her goals, dreams, and frustrations.

2. Prospective board members, talk with two or three current board members about what they enjoy about serving and what they view as the board's upcoming challenges.

3. Board members, establish a process for conducting exit interviews with board members who have resigned or otherwise completed their terms of service.

28.

What should we include
in our board orientation?

Recruiting good board members is only the beginning. To keep them informed, involved, and motivated, the board should continually evaluate itself and commit to effective board practices. Those practices begin with a comprehensive orientation for new board members.

Just before their first official meeting, and in the few weeks following, bring new board members up to speed on the organization's structure, staffing, operations, financial status, calendar of events, and other relevant activities (see Exhibit 28.1). These briefings—usually led by the board chair, governance committee chair, chief executive, or a combination of the three—may be dispersed over several weeks or grouped together in one longer session. Although newly elected members won't grasp everything immediately, they will feel more knowledgeable and therefore more comfortable when they begin participating in board business.

During the orientation, distribute copies of the board policy manual (see Question 58) and discuss its importance. Emphasize

EXHIBIT 28.1. New Board Member Orientation Checklist.

Item	By Whom?	When?
Before Election		
Organization's history and mission		
Role and expectations of board members		
Bylaws, budget, current members		
Strategic plan, major goals		
Programs and staff overview		
Soon After Election		
Facility visit and staff introductions		
Briefing on program strategies and results		
Introduction to committees and advisory groups		
Committee assignments and orientation		
Calendar of meetings and events		
Field visits (if applicable)		
Library of organizational information		
Review of audits, insurance, contracts		
Other:		
Other:		

PART
3

that the policies contained in the manual are an integral part of the board's culture, reflecting how it truly functions, not simply a list of good practices that remain in a book on the shelf. If new board members understand that following these policies is expected by their fellow members, they are more likely to do so to fit in with the existing culture.

Review the other expectations for board service, as outlined during the recruitment process. Allow time for questions and for socializing as well. When board members attend their first meeting, their learning curve will be much shorter and they will be able to recognize some familiar faces in the boardroom.

SUGGESTED ACTION STEPS

1. Board members, review your organization's orientation for new board members, ensuring that it includes a clear explanation of roles, responsibilities, and accountability.

2. Board members, if your organization does not have a formal orientation program, develop a checklist of topics to cover.

3. Board members, ask members new to the board within the last two or three years to comment on how the organization could have prepared them better for board service. Incorporate their suggestions into your organization's orientation procedures.

29

Should members of the same family serve on a board?

In general, it is not advisable to seat family members on the same board. Doing so increases the potential for internal conflict should family members vote as a block and may give donors, government agencies, or other audiences the idea that the organization does not take its public stewardship role seriously. In addition, having multiple family members on the same board tends to perpetuate a board's homogeneity (see Question 26).

Some exceptions are worth considering. For example, some nonprofit boards without term limits have benefited greatly over the years, usually in the form of significant financial gifts, from a person who is growing older. If the whole family has been involved as volunteers and donors, it would not be unusual to nurture, and then elect to the board, one of this board member's children to overlap a term or two with the parent. The assumption would be that the younger member would help sustain the family's interest for many more years, ensuring a multigenerational legacy. The same goal, however, might be achieved with sequential terms, rather than overlapping ones.

Another common example is the board of a family foundation, either operating or grantmaking. Families often hope to use board membership as a way of engaging younger generations in philanthropy. This approach may work well, depending on the individuals involved. Still, the board should be balanced with some members from outside the family, who can bring a more objective view and a different perspective to the board table.

Occasionally a board has a tradition of electing couples as members. This happens most often in local or regional charitable organizations, such as a children's home, a foster-care organization, or an organization that provides educational programs to enhance marriage. Another situation might involve a founder who, having launched an organization from the kitchen table, invites his or her spouse to serve on the board.

It would be unusual for both spouses to bring the same high level of interest and a desired expertise to the board, so nonprofits should carefully evaluate the idea of electing spouses to concurrent terms. This is especially true for small boards, which might discover that filling board slots with spouses makes it difficult to achieve diversity goals or find the skills the board needs.

If your board decides to allow members of the same family as board members, acknowledge the risks and establish clear policies to address nepotism and potential conflicts of interest (see Question 52). Those policies might include such requirements as the following:

- Family members must be able to separate their personal lives from what happens in the board room, setting aside any family conflicts or squabbles to act in the organization's best interest. Should a board member find it difficult to make a decision— say, to choose between options that are supported by different family members—he or she should feel comfortable asking to be excused from voting. The meeting minutes should make a note of the excusal from voting.

- Both spouses are expected to attend all board meetings. They should not "take turns" attending meetings or send a proxy vote with the spouse if unable to attend in person.

SUGGESTED ACTION STEPS

1. Board members, if your board has never faced this question, consider developing a policy before the situation arises.

2. Board members, if you do have family members on the board, seek a common understanding of the reasons for doing so and express those principles in a policy.

PART
3

Q&A

30.

Should constituents serve on the board?

An organization's constituents, or stakeholders—those people to whom a board feels primary accountability—should be involved in the work of the board. They might participate by serving on board committees, task forces, or advisory groups. They can feel engaged through regular communication with the organization, such as town hall meetings or focus groups in which their feedback is solicited. In some organizations, it may be appropriate for them to serve as voting members.

In membership organizations, such as trade associations, board representation is described clearly in the bylaws. The majority of the board members typically are elected by the organization members, who are the primary stakeholders. In other types of nonprofit organizations, which may have self-perpetuating or appointed boards, the board should not only define the organization's constituents but also develop ways to ensure that their voice is heard. Even primary beneficiaries of an organization's mission-related activities could be elected to the board in certain cases. For instance, health and social-service agencies might recruit current or former clients to serve on their boards.

The key is for each board to define the organization's constituency and then determine how these people should be involved with the board. It is important to remember that constituent board members need to serve the interests of the whole organization. They are not spokespersons or watchdogs for their particular interest groups.

Donors are certainly worthy of consideration for board membership, with some cautions. First, some donors are enthusiastic about the organization but not interested in serving on the board. Inviting them would put them on the spot, and they may be embarrassed to say no. Instead, invite donors to become involved in a special project or event.

PART 3

In addition, donors may not necessarily make good board members. When inviting a donor, be sure he or she fits the characteristics the board requires. You also run the risk of losing that donor's support if he or she becomes a board member and doesn't like how the board functions or the policies it adopts to guide the organization.

A board can sort out these options by assessing what expertise, skills, and personal qualities are needed to help the board do its work. Many boards develop a board profile and revise it as needed (see Question 23). This process forces the question of whether, how many, and which constituents should be considered for the board.

SUGGESTED ACTION STEPS

1. Board members, list the ways your board currently links with the organization's constituents. What other communication tools might increase constituent involvement?

2. Board members, articulate board member qualifications—based on a board profile—that will ensure adequate representation of your key constituents.

31

What should we do about uninvolved board members?

While working on the front end to recruit more committed, loyal, fully participating board members, a good board also should face up to the problem of finding a gracious way out for others. Inactive members are those who do not consistently fulfill the expectations of board service, such as attending a majority of board meetings, contributing to the work of a standing committee, and representing the organization at community or membership-related events.

Rather than allowing faithful board members to become discouraged by the inactivity of some, the board chair should call together a few board veterans to discuss the problem. Why might these board members have lost interest? Is there a personality conflict that needs to be resolved? Is there something about the board's operations or working style that is allowing decision making to be dominated by a few? Have other priorities in life taken over? Perhaps these members would prefer to resign but don't wish to appear disloyal to the organization.

When a board decides to analyze the problem of inactive board members, it may discover that poor recruitment and orientation processes were in place. In this case, the board and the individuals at issue share the problem.

The following are ways to boost the likelihood of full participation.

Institute a required rotation.   Consider amending the bylaws to require everyone to be off the board for at least one year after a certain number of years of service. This policy allows board members a periodic freedom of choice about further service. Except in larger, more complex organizations such as universities and hospitals, six years—either two three-year terms or three two-year terms—is a good length of time before a required year off (see Question 32).

Some board members will take a year off with no demonstration of continued interest at all. That signals that reelection would be a mistake for both the individual and the board. Those who want to stay involved will return rested and ready for business after the required sabbatical.

Appoint nonboard members to board committees.   If your bylaws allow this, some board members will more readily volunteer to leave the board as voting members if they can continue to serve on a board committee. Board membership may not be that important to these people, but they would like to help in a particular area of interest, such as strategic planning or finance. Absent such a provision, they may feel they need to be on the board to contribute their expertise.

Have a friendly, nonthreatening conversation.   This might be initiated by the board chair or the member who recruited the person for the board. Inactive board members won't be surprised that someone is concerned enough to say something about their absences. They have been aware (often with great guilt) of their delinquency for some time. They just didn't know how to handle the idea that they should resign. And at other times, the problem is simply a misunderstanding or a false assumption that can easily be cleared up. Usually, an agreement is made, and you either have a re-activated board member or one who feels he or she can now leave without hard feelings.

Establish a board alumni council. In organizations without re-quired term limits, a board member who is loyal to the mission and wants an ongoing affiliation may stay on the governing body be-cause there is no appropriate alternative. Some are major donors who are kept on, in spite of their inactivity, for an understandable reason. But after a decade or more on the board, the board member is probably burning out or looking for new challenges. So formalize a means for former board members to remain connected to one an-other and to the organization (see Question 33).

Establish an attendance rule with automatic termination. No one likes to fire a respected friend and volunteer, so some boards adopt a rule that says board members are automatically terminated follow-ing two or three unexcused absences. The trick is defining "unex-cused." Usually, an excused absence simply means the board member notified the chair in advance that he or she couldn't attend a meet-ing. Without these advance notifications, a no-show board member would be unexcused.

   At some point, the chair should inform the delinquent board member in writing that the board has agreed, absent an immediate request for reconsideration, that the automatic termination provi-sion should take effect.

Develop an annual affirmation statement. Just before the annual nominating and election process begins, distribute an affirmation statement for board members to sign (see Exhibit 31.1). This state-ment is a good reminder of the obligations to which a board mem-ber has committed. It also provides an opportunity to respond, "My life has changed, and I feel I can no longer serve for the coming

EXHIBIT 31.1. Board Member Annual Affirmation of Service.

1. I continue to be fully supportive of our mission, purpose, goals, and leadership.

2. I understand that board membership requires the equivalent of X days per year of my time, including preparation and meetings. I am able to give that time during the twelve months ahead, and I expect to attend all board and committee meetings unless I give the respective board chair advance notice of my need to be absent for good cause.

3. I intend to contribute financially to the work of our organization during the year and will help open doors to friends who may be interested in contributing to our work.

4. I have reviewed, signed, and intend to comply with our board's conflict-of-interest policy.

5. [Add other items important to your board.]

6. If anything should occur during the year that would not allow me to keep these intentions of being a positive contributor to our board, I will take the initiative to talk to the officers about a voluntary resignation to allow another to serve who is able to be fully involved.

Signed _____   Date _____

PART
3

year." Both the board and the individual benefit from this honesty. Everyone understands that life has many priorities, and there are no hard feelings when one opts off the board. Of course, good board members can always be reelected when their lives will allow active service again.

People are sincere when they commit to board service with the full intent to be an active member. But personal situations change. A failed business, the death of a family member, a transfer to another city—whatever the reason, board members have to look at their original commitments through a different pair of glasses. The annual statement provides that opportunity.

SUGGESTED ACTION STEPS

1. Board members, determine whether a board member's inactivity might be tied to the recruitment process. Restructure that process to prevent problems in the future.

2. Board chair, visit with a few former board members for their suggestions on how to improve board members' engagement with the organization.

3. Board members, develop an annual affirmation of board service to be signed by each board member.

32.

Should we have term limits for board members?

Term limits are an effective and natural means of keeping a board full of involved, active members. They ensure that the board keeps absorbing new enthusiasm and ideas and doesn't burn out dedicated supporters of the organization. According to research conducted by BoardSource, nearly three out of five nonprofit boards (58 percent) have term limits.

Rotating people on and off the board through term limits does the following:

- *Brings more diversity to the board.* Board members are less likely to feel as if they are filling a "token" slot when the composition of the board changes every few years (see Question 26).
- *Reinvigorates other board members.* New faces bring new perspectives and can rekindle the imagination and commitment of ongoing board members.

- *Develops new leaders.* Board service offers a different dimension of leadership that some younger or other members with the community or sector would like to experience.

- *Assures stakeholders and donors.* Boards that do not frequently welcome new members risk being seen as "insiders' clubs" or as insular in their thinking. Such attitudes can hamper fundraising and public relations efforts.

- *Reduces inactivity.* Term limits provide a built-in reason to replace board members who are passive, ineffective, troublesome, or frequently absent. There's no embarrassment associated with leaving a board once one's term ends—it's a natural transition that uninvolved board members may actually welcome as a way to depart gracefully (see Question 31).

- *Enhances the group dynamics.* Committee composition will change as new members join the board, leading to opportunities for board members to become better acquainted with people they may not have met otherwise.

Among nonprofits with term limits that were surveyed by Board-Source, most (64 percent) have three-year terms for board members. Of those organizations, two out of five (41 percent) limit the number of consecutive terms to two (for a limit of six years on the board). Some organizations set different term limits for officers.

It's best to establish a "staggered" system, with perhaps one-third of the board turning over each year. This provides some consistency among board members, which makes it easier for new board members to become familiar with the board's culture and the organization's expectations. Over time, the practices associated with term limits will become institutionalized. For example, on the basis of others' experience and the board's historical pattern of turnover, new members will expect to serve a maximum of two three-year terms. This cultural expectation will prevent them from burning out too fast or engaging too slowly in board activities. Knowing what's expected enables them to pace their participation for the maximum benefit of the organization.

Some people argue that term limits lead to a loss of expertise and organizational memory. All new board members, however, bring a special expertise to the group—perhaps one that has been lacking if board membership has been stagnant. And from the board's perspective, the organizational memory resides in the handbook of board policies revised and approved over the years (see Question 58).

SUGGESTED ACTION STEPS

1. Board members, create a policy that limits the number of consecutive years a board member can serve without a sabbatical (for example, one year off).

2. Board chair, charge the governance committee with organizing board development activities that enable new and continuing members to work together in a variety of ways.

PART
3

33.

How can we engage former board members and chief executives?

Board members who have completed their terms of office typically are among the most knowledgeable and committed of all volunteers. They are prime candidates for an ongoing relationship with the organization.

Of course, when board members voluntarily resign or leave at the end of a first term expressing no desire to be reelected, they may be signaling that something has not worked well. Confirm that assumption—maybe the former board member simply wants to be involved in a different way. Never let a former board member just drift away without a debriefing and a candid conversation about his or her desired level of continued involvement. During an exit interview or informal conversation, the board chair should ask, "What subject areas or committees interest you the most? How might the organization continue to draw on your skills?"

Here are some ways to engage former board members:

- *Recognition*. Express appreciation at the end of his or her board service by publicly presenting the person with a plaque or other gift.

- *Board committees*. Term limits might force a board member to step down from the board for at least one year. If the person has been a good board member and you think the board would want to bring him or her back in a year or two, find a useful interim assignment. If the bylaws allow it, assign an interested former board member to a board committee.

- *Emeritus status*. Some boards award emeritus status to a member who has a long and distinguished service record—but not to every former board member. An emeritus board member is generally considered to be a member for life, thereby negating any term limits or age restrictions. It is wise to clarify that the position is nonvoting; the emeritus member's attendance is often too sporadic for committee assignments and meeting quorums.

- *Board alumni council*. Some boards create a special group for former board members who wish to maintain a continued relationship with the organization. The group may even elect its own officers. Council members may occasionally be invited to board meetings as observers. The chief executive usually sends this group special mailings, highlights them in the newsletter or Web site, or provides other recognition. These friends of the organization also offer special fundraising potential.

- *Special assignments*. Appoint a former board member to lead a task force, advisory council, or special study group (see Question 18). If qualified, this person could possibly be hired as a consultant to staff.

- *Mailings*. Keep loyal volunteers informed of the organization's activities and accomplishments even after formal assignments have ended. Some chief executives continue to send board updates to former board members, often prompting a friendly idea by return mail.

PART 3

Former Chief Executives

Founding chief executives typically commit their lives to what they started. So when it comes to retirement, don't count on losing track of them. Their bodies may be weary at some point, but their commitment to see their vision fulfilled remains.

Some boards grant an emeritus title. Others make the founding, or other well-liked, chief executive a member of the board. Avoid this latter practice at all costs, because it can create real or perceived problems for the new chief executive. The board's loyalty is to the new chief executive, who may have been selected for different reasons than the previous chief executive (see Question 69).

If the new staff leader welcomes the continued involvement of one or more former chief executives, he or she should make that determination, not the board. The current chief executive, for example, may decide to retain his or her predecessor on a part-time basis to provide continuity with major donors. After all, experts say it takes up to five years to nurture a person of wealth to make a major gift. The former chief executive, however, may find it difficult to be accountable to the current one in terms of goals, working conditions, and compensation. In addition, staff and board members, clients, and others may be tempted to turn to the person they've known longer, out of habit. This undermines the authority of the new chief executive and can cause significant organizational problems.

The best situation is for the former chief executive to simply say goodbye to the organization. At a much later date—and only at the current chief executive's invitation—the former chief executive may become involved in some aspect of the organization's work.

SUGGESTED ACTION STEPS

1. Board chair, conduct exit interviews with departing board members, in person or by phone, to gauge their feelings about their service.

2. Board chair, set aside ten minutes during a board meeting to brainstorm about ways to engage former board members and chief executives.

34.

Should board members
be compensated?

Although nonprofit board service is usually a volunteer activity, reasonable fees for service are permissible if the bylaws state so or the majority of the board members so determine. However, such compensation is rare. According to a survey conducted by BoardSource, board service remains voluntary in the vast majority of responding organizations; only 2 percent provide board members with a fee or honorarium for their service.

Board compensation is more common in complex nonprofits, such as health care systems or large foundations. Many organizations believe a fee is appropriate when the responsibilities of board members are particularly time-consuming or when legal requirements make the service unusually demanding. Also, compensation can make it possible for individuals of very limited financial means to participate in board service.

According to the basic tenets of nonprofit law, directors and officers should not make any pecuniary (monetary) profit from the organization, and they should not receive personal financial benefit from their association with the organization. Paying a fee in specific circumstances can be defended, but fees that are out of scale with the market price of that good or service are always unacceptable. Excessive compensation can be a cause for a fine or for the organization to lose its tax-exempt status (see Question 7).

Tying board service to monetary benefits can cloud board members' judgment by tempting them to make decisions based on personal interest rather than what is best for the organization. To avoid even a perception of personal gain, the board might want to have compensation determinations made by a task force of appropriate outsiders or a board committee whose members lack conflict of interest with respect to the arrangement.

Following are some common situations with board members that call for the development and implementation of clear policies.

Reimbursement of expenses.   Traveling to a distant board meeting can become a major expense. Not every board member has equal financial capacity to absorb those costs. But paying for plane tickets, hotel accommodations, and meals, even in part, can become a substantial expense for the nonprofit.

Clarify the reimbursement policy for potential board members, emphasizing that board service should not cause personal economic hardship. Spell out, for example, whether the organization will not reimburse any expenses or will reimburse some or all expenses (up to a certain limit or according to a per-diem calculation). According to the BoardSource survey, 24 percent of the respondents' organizations reimburse board members for the expenses they incur in attending meetings.

Business relationships with board members.   Board members often recommend their own business services to the organization on whose board they serve. It is not inappropriate for a nonprofit organization to have business relationships with board members, provided ethical procedures are followed, such as full disclosure of conflicts of interest (see Question 52). The organization needs to openly seek bids to procure services, keeping in mind that what is best for the organization must be the determining factor.

Sometimes a board member is willing to provide services at a discount. In that case, the minutes should document that the final decision was made in the best interests of the nonprofit and that the board was aware of the potential conflict.

Board members wearing two hats. Often during the beginning phase in the life of an organization, the board may have two functions: it acts as the governing body while at the same time fulfilling the duties of staff members. In some arts organizations, for example, board members also act as directors or producers. In some hospitals, board members may also be physicians.

Such situations complicate the issue of accountability. Being compensated for staff activities while simultaneously serving as a volunteer overseer of the organization may create confusion between the two responsibilities (see Question 62). Board members may need to determine which activity they prefer to pursue—being part of the staff or of the board. Or they may excuse themselves from some decisions (often with prompting from the chair or chief executive about their conflicting interests).

Donors' expectations. Funders or individual donors generally expect their contributions to go to programs and services. The board should take into account possible reactions from funders and donors before it begins accepting compensation for board service.

Each board member should answer this question: "How does my commitment change if I am paid for the service?" Sometimes the time and monetary burden can be too demanding without any compensation. In that case, before accepting the commitment or before lowering the standards of promised involvement, it is important to communicate these concerns to the chair of the board. The best solution may be for the board member to rotate off the board.

PART
3

SUGGESTED ACTION STEPS

1. Board members, if you are considering providing compensation to the board, conduct the appropriate market research to find out how many nonprofits in your area pay board members for their board work and how much board members receive.

2. Board chair, because board members are looking for personal, intangible rewards, take ten minutes of a board meeting to talk about the adequacy of those rewards.

PART 3

Q_A 35.

Should board members be evaluated periodically?

No individual or organization develops excellence without setting standards and submitting to some measure of accountability. Evaluations of staff performance, for instance, are usually done annually. Board members should be no exception. If they are committed to good governance, board members will create a climate in which an evaluation process is seen as a natural way to improve how the board functions.

Following are suggestions for making board member evaluation a regular and productive part of board service.

Determine the criteria. Your policies should include a job description for the board, expectations of board members, and a profile of the desired qualities of new board members (see Question 23), all approved by the board. Before their election, board members should know what's expected of them, such as attending a majority of board meetings, assisting in fundraising initiatives, preparing in advance for board meetings, and representing the organization in the broader community (see Question 1). The evaluation criteria do not represent a checklist of what a particular board member has or hasn't done but rather serve as a reminder of the goals he or she should be striving for.

Assign the evaluation task. A subgroup of the board, usually the governance committee, should facilitate the process. Evaluation fits with the committee's other tasks of nominating board members for election or reelection, orienting new members, and planning board education activities.

Create a consistent process. When evaluation is routine rather than provoked by a crisis or uproar from a few, the task is less emotional and builds credibility. Because some board members usually end their terms each year, an evaluation will be useful in determining whether an individual should be reelected. Conduct evaluations at the same time each year so that board members come to expect the exercise.

Promote self-evaluation. Since the purpose of board member evaluation is to improve individual performance—and thus the performance of the board itself—self-evaluation must be part of the process. Some boards use a simple format asking people to rate themselves on ten items or so using a 1 to 5 scale. Others use an annual affirmation statement as part of this annual process (see Question 31), although this statement addresses commitment rather than effectiveness.

Maintain confidentiality. Only the board committee conducting the evaluation should see all the responses, submitted anonymously by board members. Committee members should report back to the entire board in general terms, offering recommendations to address any areas of concern, such as a high percentage of board members who report that they do not review advance materials in great depth.

Provide individual feedback. For some board members, a confidential phone call from the committee chair satisfies the desire to know how well he or she is doing in the eyes of others. For others, the self-evaluation survey will suffice. All feedback should be based on criteria known to and applied to every board member.

Leverage the information. Use what you learn to make improvements. For instance, the governance committee can use the information gathered to develop a better description of board member expectations, a stronger orientation program for new board members, and a plan for board training.

Boards without term limits should be most open to individual evaluation because their members tend to be reelected repeatedly, often without consideration of individual performance. Ideally, the self-evaluation process should be used routinely and consistently as a board development tool that can add to the organization's long-term strength. Develop a process that fits the organization's culture, so that people feel comfortable being introspective.

PART
3

SUGGESTED ACTION STEPS

1. Board chair, ask board members who have served on boards that did individual evaluation to comment on their experiences.

2. Board chair, ask the governance committee to draft a proposal for board member evaluation and bring it to the board for discussion.

3. Board members, develop quick methods by which you can informally evaluate your own individual performance throughout the year, such as a short e-mail questionnaire sent by the board chair. These might include questions such as, How clear is the organization's mission to you? How clear is your role on the board to you?

36.

How can our board assess and improve its own performance?

A large part of a board's role is monitoring the organization's overall performance. Is the organization carrying out its mission effectively? Is it fulfilling its legal requirements? Are financial policies being followed? But the full board should also assess its own performance in guiding the organization. The full board, acting as a unified body, has a responsibility for ethical, moral, and fiduciary oversight that is greater than the individual board members' responsibilities. Even when board members have engaged in a self-evaluation process as individuals (see Question 35), they still need to look at the board's functioning as a whole. Following are some reasons why:

- A nonprofit organization, in the long run, is no better than its board. It is in everyone's interest to help the board function as effectively as it possibly can. Through these efforts, the organization will also improve.

- Individual board members become frustrated when they perceive that the overall board is dysfunctional in key areas. As a result, attendance at or participation in board meetings drops.

- Staff morale suffers when the board doesn't seem cohesive, efficient, or productive. Staff members' trust and respect for the board wanes, and few chief executives on their own can fill that leadership vacuum.

- When a board can address its own needs honestly, it sends the right message to staff members, that making mistakes and learning from them is natural and expected.

- An effective board addresses issues, keeps the mission clear, uses funds wisely, and makes board meetings enjoyable. New member recruitment becomes easy because others want to join a winning team.

PART
3

Evaluation Tools

A formal assessment of the full board's functions and ability to work well as a group should be conducted every three or four years. The process of asking, "How are we doing?" might be tied to the strategic planning process or spurred by the upcoming retirement of a long-standing chair or the departure of the chief executive. It is best to schedule the evaluation for a retreat or a special board meeting, rather than undertake it when the organization is in crisis or experiencing personnel issues within the board.

You can also undertake informal evaluations to help the board stay focused on self-improvement, using one or more of the techniques outlined as follows.

Regular board discussions. Put on each board meeting agenda a ten- to fifteen-minute item called "Ideas for Improving Our Board." The board chair should be a champion of board improvement. The morale and loyalty of board members are stronger when the board is given the freedom to make suggestions. However, frank discussion also raises expectations that things will change. When a consensus is evident, the chair must be prepared to take action or refer ideas to a committee or task force for further consideration.

Board trainings. These can provide the stimulus for taking an in-depth look at board members' roles, individually or collectively. A session or two of board training—using a book, an outline, a veteran board member, or a consultant—can help set standards against which the board can measure its own performance.

Board surveys. Typically, a board self-evaluation survey is a confidential questionnaire that asks board members to rate how well the board does in various areas. The questions, usually rated on a numerical scale, might include the following:

- How effective is the board's decision-making process?
- How effective is the board's strategic planning process?
- How productive are the board committees?
- What is the quality of communication among board members, between board and staff, and from other stakeholders to board members?

You can also invite written comments by including a lead-in phrase such as, "If I could change three things about how this board operates, they would be . . ." (You don't necessarily need to develop your own evaluation tool; organizations such as BoardSource and various associations have developed assessment instruments specifically for nonprofit boards.)

The board receives a summary of the responses—which should be tabulated by a nonboard member or consultant—but respondents' names are not mentioned. You'll end up with a candid summary of what the board does well and where it could stand improvement. For instance, the findings may point to board members' desire to make better use of their time, focus more on meaningful issues rather than administrative tasks, interact more with one another, or simply enjoy their positions more.

External audits. On occasion, your board may wish to engage an expert on governance to facilitate a more thorough evaluation of its governance practices. Typically, an external audit includes reviewing the articles of incorporation and bylaws; observing board and committee meetings; and interviewing officers, other board members, former board members, and the chief executive. The external consultant may also create and administer a mail or in-meeting survey and then facilitate a board discussion about key issues that emerged from the survey.

PART
3

By contracting with an expert who knows how other boards function, a board improves its chances of focusing on positive changes and increases its own level of interest and participation. A consultant is more objective than a member of the board and can offer alternatives for addressing problems. In addition, employing an external consultant is usually less threatening than having your own leaders conduct a peer evaluation.

The board as a whole should discuss the findings of an evaluation and what can be done to improve its effectiveness or productivity. For instance, the results of a self-evaluation may prompt the board to consider making some governance changes, such as reducing the number of standing committees, or to modify its communication practices with board members. It is impossible to complete an evaluation and deal constructively with all options for change in a single meeting. Allow enough time to do a thorough job— approximately six to nine months for the entire process.

Aside from a formal evaluation every three or four years, ongoing ways that board members can evaluate the organization's performance include

- Developing a board calendar that includes the chief executive's evaluation, a board self-assessment, and a review of mission, vision, and objectives (see Questions 3 and 63).

- Scheduling a board retreat every year or two to reflect on the mission and overall board functioning and to engage in the strategic planning process (see Question 40).

- Approving performance objectives tied to each part of the strategic plan, including targeted results and a timetable for achieving them.

- Reviewing financial results and other measurable outcomes with an eye toward ending those that do not contribute to a healthy bottom line (see Question 47).

- Understanding that performance assessment, in itself, is not productive unless accompanied by concerted efforts to react to the results and implement changes.

SUGGESTED ACTION STEPS

1. Board chair, take five minutes during a meeting to ask each board member to rank, on a scale of 1 to 10, how effective he or she thinks the governance process is.

2. Chief executive, budget for training publications or tapes, consultant fees and expenses, retreat expenses, supplies and materials, and other costs associated with evaluation.

3. Board members, commit to one three-hour training session with a trainer who specializes in working with nonprofits. Prepare a follow-up agenda for board development over the next year or two.

4. Board members, develop a schedule for board evaluation.

PART FOUR

Board and
Committee Meetings

A part of joining a board is the expectation of making a meaningful contribution. That is most likely to happen when meetings of board members deal with the "big issues"—the strategic actions the organization must take to achieve its mission. Committees usually focus on a particular strategic area, such as finances or governance, but they too should not stray from their charge to provide the board with recommendations for guidelines and direction setting.

Board meetings should be all about governance and high-level decision making, not the administrative or operational matters that rightfully are the chief executive's responsibility. The board chair is the key figure in keeping the board focused on its governance role, although all board members should feel comfortable in pointing out when discussions have strayed into operational areas that are not their responsibility. At the committee level, committee chairs play the same leadership role.

Beyond attending meetings and doing the homework for them, serving on a board is about productive, enjoyable interactions with peers. Building and strengthening those peer relationships, during formal as well as informal gatherings of board members, will build and strengthen the board itself.

Q&A

37.

Is a board legally required to hold open meetings?

All states have "sunshine" laws. Alternatively known as open meeting laws, these regulations are intended to shed light on the inner workings of an organization and promote accountability by those in decision-making positions. Proponents believe that sunshine laws increase accountability by bringing board decisions out from behind closed doors. Some boards, however, feel that having outsiders in a meeting detracts from the spirit of open debate, especially when a potentially controversial issue is on the agenda.

In general, the laws pertain to state governments and nonprofits that receive public funds (such as school boards). Some states have extended sunshine laws to cover nonprofits that have government contracts or have government officials serving on their board (which may be a condition of the funding). Those affected by sunshine laws usually must satisfy certain requirements for notifying the public about meetings, making meeting locations accessible, and providing minutes of the meetings within a reasonable time.

The laws do not prohibit closed meetings when certain issues are under discussion, such as salaries, lawsuits, disciplinary actions, personnel matters, or business negotiations. On the contrary, confidential matters must be handled in private in order not to reveal anyone's personal information or jeopardize the organization's business plans. In general, nonprofit board meetings are considered private business meetings, and the board can determine who attends. If your board issues an invitation to outside observers, it may make sense to schedule time for a question-and-answer session at the end of the meeting. That will help prevent the observers from interrupting or disturbing the proceedings.

Even if your organization is not subject to sunshine laws, making efforts to operate in an open, accountable manner can increase public confidence in and support of your mission. That means intentionally providing the interested public with information on which it can evaluate your organization's performance, whether it's posting your Form 990 on your Web site (see Question 54) or issuing an open invitation for people to attend board meetings.

The public often seeks such openness, or transparency, in regard to financial decisions. Your organization's stakeholders may also desire to know more about internal processes: How are leaders chosen? How are decisions made? How are plans and objectives established? Making nonconfidential information readily available—even if someone is not specifically asking for it—can reduce any suspicions that may arise among staff, donors, the media, and even other board members. By being forthcoming with information, you prove yourself worthy of the public's trust.

SUGGESTED ACTION STEPS

1. Board members, look for ways in which your organization and its board can operate in a more transparent manner, such as posting nonconfidential information on a Web site and willingly sharing information when requested.

2. Board chair, ask other organizations about their practices to promote transparency, and consult with your legal counsel as well.

38.

How often and where should we meet?

Board members often feel pressed for time. They don't necessarily prefer to spend days attending a meeting on the other side of the country or even hours driving across town.

Streamlining board governance often includes reducing the number of board meetings and making each meeting more efficient through the use of consent agendas, the absence of routine committee reports, and a focus on major organizational matters rather than operational issues (see Question 39).

A board should meet only as many times as are required to fulfill its role. According to a survey by BoardSource, the largest percentage of boards (41 percent) meets monthly. One in four boards (25 percent) meets bimonthly, with a similar percentage meeting quarterly (24 percent).

Most state laws require an annual meeting at which board members and officers are elected and other necessary business is carried out. Few boards, however, can fulfill their fiduciary duties adequately by meeting only once a year. It may be necessary to meet monthly in the first phase of organizational life, then reduce the frequency to whatever is appropriate for each following phase of the organization's lifecycle. National or international organizations may convene their boards only a few times per year, although the meetings may last a full two days, and then communicate via conference call or electronically between meetings.

Technology can improve communications and reduce the number of live meetings necessary to get the same amount of work done (see Question 46). Some organizations, for example, keep the same number of meetings but don't always hold them face to face. They might hold half of their annual meetings in person and half via audioconference. Others use private online forums or listservs that allow for discussion and informal consensus in advance of the official meeting.

As for the physical setting of a board meeting, it should be conducive to large-group work. Perhaps the conference room at the organization's headquarters fills that bill—but a change of scenery once in a while can spark new ways of thinking among board members.

PART 4

Here are some inventive ways and places to hold board meetings:

- A city hall hearing room for a briefing on demographic and economic trends
- A tour of the organization's facility with several "briefing stops" along the way
- A visit to a program site where the organization is working
- A retreat center in tranquil surroundings conducive to strategic thinking
- A place to observe staff members serving the primary beneficiaries of the organization
- A high-tech conference room at a local business
- A bus tour of sites being served by the organization, with business conducted on the bus

The objective is to make the meeting memorable. Even if the board meeting takes place in a drab conference room, it might include the following:

- Informal time for fellowship.
- Staff presentations on specific programs or initiatives.
- Committee meetings held before or after. (Board members who are already onsite for a board meeting may appreciate this efficiency. The committee, however, should not prepare any resolutions or recommendations for the board meeting immediately following.)
- Governance training, including board self-assessment.
- The opportunity to meet and mingle with staff, clients, and vendors.
- Briefings on the environment in which the organization operates, including other nonprofits, the community, and the local economy.
- Bulletin boards with special displays.
- Business sessions for formal decisions.
- Brainstorming sessions to think about emerging trends and the organization's future.
- An executive session.

SUGGESTED ACTION STEPS

1. Board chair, ask each board member to write down how many meetings per year seem ideal for the organization at this stage in its lifecycle. Average the number and discuss the results.

2. Board members, at least once a year, hold a board meeting in a different or unique location.

PART
4

39

How can we improve our meetings?

It's rewarding to serve on a board when you feel valued as a member and when the group accomplishes much in a few hours. Everyone likes meetings that feature good preparation, open discussion, clear consensus, and quick follow-up. Following are ten tips for better board meetings.

Build on the basics. Make sure you have all the required elements in place: a clear mission statement and organizational goals, committed board members with defined roles, and good communication between the board chair and the chief executive.

Plan meetings well in advance. Plan the board's calendar one year ahead, and reserve a meeting location. The board chair and the chief executive should set the agenda and check in with committee chairs to determine whether a particular committee will require board action on any recommendations or will simply provide informational reports. Allow enough time to distribute materials and reports before the meeting so all board members can come prepared to do business.

Provide a positive environment. Make sure the meeting's location has good lighting and ventilation, comfortable seats, and enough space for members to spread out their materials. Limit distractions as much as possible.

Pay attention to logistical details. Staff members typically coordinate the many details that make a meeting go off without a hitch. These include providing written directions to the meeting location, the right audiovisual equipment, refreshments, name cards on the table and name tags that are easily read at a distance, a seating arrangement that allows board members and the chief executive to see one another around a table, and places for staff members to sit.

Manage the meeting effectively. A strong presiding board chair is absolutely essential to an effective meeting (see Question 19). When the meeting is managed with a firm yet respectful hand, the participants will feel that their time has been well spent and they have made a real contribution. The chair needs to provide structure—such as ensuring that the meeting starts and ends on time— yet should take care not to stifle debate and discussion.

PART
4

Follow the agenda. A good meeting follows the written agenda, allowing ample time for discussion and possibly a presentation by an outside speaker or other board training segment. To free up time for strategic thinking and discussion, begin the meeting agenda with a consent calendar, or consent agenda. This agenda item groups routine, noncontroversial, and self-explanatory issues under one umbrella so they can be acted upon as an entire package.

The issues included in a consent agenda do not require discussion before being voted on and typically include acceptance of committee reports and previous board meeting minutes, routine correspondence, and minor changes or updates to policy documents. Board members should receive the consent agenda support documents in the board packets well in advance of the meeting and, once at the meeting, feel comfortable asking that an item be taken off the agenda so it can be discussed by the full board.

Here's a sample agenda:

- Welcome and comments from the chair
- Consent agenda
    Minutes of the previous board meeting
    Fundraising committee report
    Chief executive's report
- Strategic discussions
    Presentation by outside consultant
    Discussion of emerging trends and opportunities
- Governance committee discussions
    Recruitment of new board members
    Board self-assessment
- Executive session with auditor

PART 4

Allow adequate time for discussion. In advance, board members should agree on time limits for some discussion items. When the board is deliberating critical policies, hold the discussion at one meeting and then take action at the next. Set aside time for board members to ask questions about the written staff reports mailed in advance.

Streamline the meeting with sound preparation. The chief executive and the staff should mail reports and the consent agenda two weeks in advance of the board meeting. They should also anticipate other materials that might be needed. Past minutes, bylaws, the annual audit, the list of property owned, and other items can be kept in a loose-leaf board reference book for use during meetings. Other handouts might contain draft language for complicated resolutions or the pros and cons of a proposed policy, based on input from committee chairs.

Hold an executive session without staff. All board members deserve a regular opportunity to speak frankly without staff members or guests present. The best way to defuse misunderstandings or head off a problem before it becomes serious is to provide a routine time for the board to meet alone. Usually an executive session works best as the last agenda item. These sessions may last only five or ten minutes—whatever is necessary to address the issue at hand. In addition, before the general meeting some boards meet first with their chief executive in an informal, nonthreatening manner to allow airing of overall or specific concerns that "keep the president awake at night" (often referred to by the acronym KPAWN).

Start follow-up immediately after the meeting. Good meetings include immediate follow-up: thank-you letters, minutes, assignment of policy decisions, staff briefings, and a phone debriefing between the board chair and the chief executive. The chief executive gains credibility when he or she sends a memo to the board one week after a meeting to explain how the staff is implementing recent board decisions.

PART
4

Committee Meetings

Most boards operate with a few standing committees and create special committees or task forces to function for specific times on more focused issues. These groups may be strategic in nature or action-oriented (for example, related to an important event or function).

Remember that board committees are created to help the board do its work, not to oversee staff work (see Questions 15 and 16). The finance committee, for example, must resist getting so deeply into the details that it loses track of its broader role: to help the board adopt sound parameters guiding staff actions in the finance area.

Many of the suggestions for improving board meetings apply to committee meetings as well. The following differences apply, however:

- The specific purpose and responsibilities of each committee should be outlined in the standing policies of the board. These written policies should cover the committee's job description, who appoints the chair, the chair's term limit, inclusion of non-board members as committee members, and staff assistance.

- No federal or state laws govern how committees operate, how often they must meet, or what records they must keep. Those decisions are up to the committee chairs. Some might prefer a set schedule and structured face-to-face meetings, while others will convene meetings by phone, communicate primarily through e-mail, and keep informal notes instead of formal minutes.

- Any resolutions approved by the committee must be forwarded to the full board for action. The committee chair should communicate immediately with the chief executive and board chair regarding committee items for the next board agenda. It's also a good practice for the committee chair to periodically submit a report to the board that summarizes the committee's findings, accomplishments, and recommendations.

Informal Meetings

Informal meetings between the board chair and the chief executive, or a few members of a committee before a full committee meeting, can keep things on track. But avoid the situation in which a few people, getting together for lunch or coffee, conduct official business. That leaves the full board uninformed and out of the decision-making loop; matters requiring formal board approval are then left out of the organization's record, which can have legal ramifications.

To make informal meetings productive, do the following:

- Make the purpose of the meeting clear to all participants.
- Assign someone to take the lead role in guiding conversations.
- Assign a participant to follow up on the areas of conclusion.
- Document the meeting in written form, if appropriate.
- Inform others who need to know the results of the meeting.

Social Gatherings

Good board policies flow from mutual respect, trust, and loyalty among board members and between board members and the staff. A board builds these qualities best through interaction outside the board room.

Time spent in a relaxed setting—at the home of the chief executive or a board member, on the tennis court or golf course, at a picnic—contributes to good working relationships. Usually a few board members are good at helping the group bond through these informal times. Take advantage of their gifts of hospitality, humor, or creative ideas for group interaction. Involve families, if possible, for they provide the support that enables board members to devote occasional weekends and evenings to board service.

PART
4

SUGGESTED ACTION STEPS

1. Chief executive, survey board members to find out how meetings could be improved. Provide a summary of the results and adopt some of the suggested changes.

2. Board members, develop criteria for selecting the board and committee chairs that include proven ability to plan and preside at meetings.

3. Chief executive, be sure staff members are assigned to each committee and know their boundaries in working with committee chairs.

Q A

40.

How is a retreat different from a board meeting?

Sometimes board members need to step away from the organization to get a better look at the bigger picture. A retreat offers them the opportunity to delve more deeply into strategic issues that they may not always have time to address during regular board meetings.

Free from the regular business of governing, board members can turn their attention to long-term questions such as, What developing trends will shape the organization in the next five to ten years? Where do we as an organization want to be in five years? Whom do we want to be serving? How will we know if we have succeeded? What can we do now to increase our chances of success in the future? They can revisit the organization's mission and vision, possibly in preparation for the development or revision of a strategic plan (see Questions 3 and 4).

Many organizations schedule an annual retreat, which might include team-building exercises, orientation for new board members, a refresher course on board members' roles and responsibilities, or self-assessment exercises. However, a retreat isn't just a productive time for long-term, strategic thinking but also an opportunity to get to know the chief executive and staff outside of the working environment. It includes social interaction, so encourage all board members to dress casually and comfortably.

Ideally, the schedule for an annual board retreat should include lots of time for informal discussions during meals and refreshment breaks. Board members can take walks, play golf, or simply enjoy one another's company as they talk informally about the future and how the organization will deal with it.

Despite the informal environment of a board retreat, it still requires a lot of advance planning.

To make the most of board members' valuable time, the retreat should have a well-defined purpose and clear objectives, be scheduled far enough in advance to enable most people to participate, and feature knowledgeable presenters. You might retain a consultant to facilitate discussions or lead group exercises, which frees up the chief executive and board chair to participate more fully in the retreat.

PART
4

SUGGESTED ACTION STEPS

1. Board chair, ask whether the board would like to substitute a retreat (with at least one overnight) for one regular meeting.

2. Board members, at least every two or three years, plan and budget for a board retreat that includes social activities.

41.

Who should attend board meetings and what are their roles?

The simple answer to this question is to invite as many people as will improve the organization's governance and mission. Each meeting might have different participants, selected from the following possibilities.

- *Board members.* Every board member should make it a priority to attend every meeting.

- *Chief executive.* The board chair and the chief executive should sit next to one another during business sessions, working as a team. The chief executive usually is a nonvoting member of the board.

- *Senior staff members.* Those who report to the chief executive and serve as staff aides to committees should be invited to most board meetings. They should be prepared to provide information when called on by the chief executive. In general, other staff members attend board meetings only for special purposes, such as presenting the results of a study to the board or providing administrative support to the chief executive.

- *Auditor.* A representative of the firm that performed the external audit can provide a brief report to the board and answer general questions about the organization's finances. (More pointed questions should be addressed to the auditor during an executive session without the chief executive present.)

- *Guest presenters.* An attorney, an architect, a consultant who has just evaluated the organization's fundraising operation, or a similar outside expert may be invited for a specific time slot in the agenda. He or she is introduced, gives a short presentation, responds to questions, and then is thanked and excused from the meeting.

- *Board trainer.* Some boards occasionally invite an outside person—a former board member or a consultant—to monitor their meetings and provide feedback on how they can improve. Usually, this person sits apart from the board table, observes, and takes five minutes at the end to make helpful comments. The board trainer may meet with the board chair and chief executive alone to provide additional recommendations for their roles.

- *Prospective board members.* Observing an actual board meeting can help candidates for board membership make a final decision. In turn, the board has the opportunity to meet a potential peer.

- *Prospective major donors.* Before agreeing to make a major contribution, a donor might ask to sit in on a board meeting. If you acquiesce, understand the inherent risk. The content and effectiveness of the meeting can convince the donor either to partner with your organization or to look elsewhere.

- *Primary beneficiaries.* Perhaps there are people your organization serves who would be honored to tell their stories to the

PART
4

board. This enables the board to see and hear firsthand the results of the organization's efforts. Schedule these participants for a specific time—perhaps over lunch, to allow for personal interaction with board members.

- *Emeritus board members.* Some boards grant this honorary title to a few distinguished board alumni. Other boards create an alumni council for all board members who served more than a specified number of years (see Question 33).

The board may decide who attends board meetings, with one significant exception. All states have open meeting laws—sometimes called sunshine laws—that principally apply to organizations receiving government funding. These laws vary from state to state, but the principle is to promote public accountability, ensuring that important decisions relating to the use of taxpayer dollars are known and allowing interested constituents to observe the decision-making process (see Question 37).

SUGGESTED ACTION STEPS

1. Board chair, ask each board member, confidentially, whether he or she feels comfortable with the people who usually attend meetings.

2. Board members, take five minutes to brainstorm about whom you would like to include on your agenda at the next few meetings.

42.

How should staff members participate in board and committee meetings?

In addition to working closely with the board chair on substantive preparation in advance of a meeting, the chief executive plays several roles once the meeting begins. He or she

- Provides information the board needs to govern. The chief executive is in the best position to bring the necessary insider's perspective to the discussion.
- Answers all questions raised by board members, or calls on the appropriate staff members in the room to provide the requested information.
- Helps the board chair manage the meeting productively. Often, the board chair and the chief executive sit next to one another for ease of communication.

- Helps board members feel positive about their service to the organization, perhaps by arranging for special recognition or a gift of appreciation.

Other senior staff members play an important role in board meetings, but they fulfill this role primarily before the board arrives for the meeting. For example, they guide and support the committees for which they serve as the staff liaisons, and they prepare written reports and briefings for the board. The chief executive should approve these reports before they are sent to board members in advance of meetings.

During board meetings, senior staff members should

- Give presentations on their areas of responsibility, as requested by the chief executive or board chair. For example, the chief financial officer may give the financial report and brief the board on the budget.

- Respond to requests for information during or after the meeting, when requested by the chief executive. The provision of too many operational details, however, can sidetrack board members from focusing on larger strategic issues and policy development.

- Demonstrate their support of the chief executive and the management team and reflect loyalty to the organization and its mission. Board members pick up signals about the status of the organization as they watch and talk with staff members.

- Interact with board members during refreshment breaks and meals.

The board may formally elect or designate one staff member—often the assistant to the chief executive—to serve as the board secretary. The person in this position typically sends board communications, arranges travel, makes sure the room is set up properly, and handles other meeting logistics. If the board secretary is also responsible for drafting the board minutes, he or she must attend every board meeting, except for the executive session portion.

Staff Members as Board Members

It is common for the chief executive—but no other staff member— to serve ex officio as a board member. In fact, the chief executive is the only staff member who should serve on the board. Some people advocate voting rights for the chief executive to reflect a true peer relationship while working with the board. Others believe the chief executive should be a nonvoting board member because of the inevitable conflicts of interest (see Question 61).

As for other staff members, there are too many conflicts of interest inherent in their election to the board. For instance, it would put them in the strange position of acting as the chief executive's employer—since the chief executive reports to the board—while at the same time reporting to that same chief executive as an employee. As board members, they would approve budget expenditures that, as staff members, they would oversee—a situation that would make it impossible to be objective stewards of the organization at the governance level. In fact, watchdog and umbrella associations recommend against such "inside" board members, with the exception of the chief executive.

There is also a risk that volunteer board members will depend on the knowledge of staff board members and never fully exercise their own governance roles. An all-volunteer board learns more easily the distinction between board work and staff work. Because senior staff members typically attend board meetings, the board can still benefit from the staff members' experience and perspectives without putting them on the board.

In addition, board membership for some staff members but not others can create divisions within the organization. It would give some people authority over their peers in decisions about budget, salaries and benefits, and program priorities.

PART
4

As the backbone of nonprofit organizations, boards are accountable for stewardship of the public's investment in their charitable mission. For-profit corporations routinely put paid executives on their boards. Nonprofits need to pursue good business practices, but they are not pursuing profits. They are changing lives and providing services. In exchange, they receive contributions and tax benefits. Accountability to an organization's stakeholders calls for a separation of power, a set of checks and balances that comes from distinguishing the role of the board from that of the staff.

SUGGESTED ACTION STEPS

1. Chief executive, ask board members what they think staff members could do to improve committee meetings.

2. Chief executive, invite staff members to brainstorm about how they could improve the next board meeting.

3. Board members, review the organization's bylaws and policies to determine whether they need to more explicitly state whether staff members can serve on the board.

4. Board chair, if a few board members are championing a staff member for board election, find out what they believe that person will bring to the group; identify other candidates who would bring similar expertise or characteristics as well as an outsider's objectivity.

43.

What are the different ways boards make decisions?

You might be surprised at the range of decision-making methods used by nonprofit boards. Some follow Robert's Rules of Order to the letter, while others take a less rigid approach to the governance process. Whatever the voting process used, spell it out in the bylaws and make sure it is fair and open and calls for decisions to be recorded.

Many small decisions—such as meeting locations, agendas, advance materials, and board reports—are made legitimately for the board by the board chair or the chief executive. For policy and governance decisions, boards may take one of the following approaches.

Simple majority vote. In this classic method, the chair either asks for a voice vote, declaring his or her sense of the majority subject to objection, or asks for a show of hands. Even when a vote seems unanimous, the board chair should guard against rattling off, "All in favor say aye; all opposed no; the ayes have it; the motion is passed" without ever looking up from his or her notes. Even quick, unanimous votes should reflect legitimate agreement after much discussion of the options.

Supermajority vote. Some decisions—amending the bylaws, firing the chief executive, or approving real estate transactions, for example—require more than a simple majority. Sometimes the preference is for two-thirds, sometimes for three-fourths. The bylaws might outline other important decisions that should require a supermajority.

A related question is the definition of a quorum. A quorum requirement of only one-third of the board members, followed by a simple majority, enables very few board members to make decisions. At the opposite end of the spectrum, a two-thirds quorum might be required for important business such as hiring or firing a chief executive.

PART
4

Consensus. This word has numerous interpretations. It is not synonymous with "unanimous decision" or "compromise." Technically speaking, consensus is a tedious, time-consuming process that phrases and rephrases a decision to eventually satisfy all of the parties involved. True consensus requires high-level facilitation skills and the patience to craft numerous iterations of the same decision or resolution. At the end, all participants feel comfortable they can live with the decision.

A consensus can also be used as a condition for taking a vote. After what he or she thinks has been adequate discussion, the chair might ask, "Is there consensus (total agreement) that it's time to vote?" That is a signal for those who have been holding back to have their say.

Unanimity only. Some boards, especially some in particular religious traditions, believe it is important to reach unanimity before finalizing any board action. To succeed, this approach requires the support of a special culture. The spirit of this approach is admirable, but it rarely works well. First, some would argue that the whole reason for having a group of nine, fifteen, or twenty-one board members is to bring a diversity of views to the table. The practice of required unanimity tends to silence those who would otherwise take a different view. Others may feel unspoken pressure to go along with the perceived majority at the time of voting, only to feel like a hypocrite later.

In most board cultures, unanimity is not typical. In fact, if all of its decisions are unanimous, a board probably has other problems such as uninvolved board members or confusion about roles and responsibilities. A board can still enjoy unity while encouraging board members to speak and vote their true conscience. In other words, a board can have unity without unanimity on all votes.

Some boards use a mix of approaches: they might require a majority vote on routine matters, a supermajority on some issues, and unanimity on the most critical issues.

PART
4

Open Voting Versus Secret Ballot

In most cases, open voting is preferable for nonprofit boards. Even when a board goes into executive session, its members still see who votes how. This approach creates trust over the long run. One exception, on some boards, is the practice of choosing board officers by secret ballot.

SUGGESTED ACTION STEPS

1. Board chair, ask your legal adviser to suggest how the bylaws could reflect good decision-making practices that others use.

2. Board chair, put the topic of decision making on the agenda for the next meeting of the governance committee.

Q A

44.

What if a board member opposes a board decision?

Disagreements within the boardroom are proper and expected, as long as everyone models for one another how to disagree agreeably. Board members need to separate the policy difference from the person. How a board member expresses disagreement is often more important than the difference of opinion itself. But once everyone has had a fair chance to debate the issue, the board should act, and those in the minority should stop airing their objections.

Following are some reasons for which board members may disagree:

- *Lack of clarity.* An issue that was never expressed clearly is subject to different interpretations. The solution is to redraft the resolution or policy so that any reasonable person will interpret it correctly.

- *Lack of guidance.* One persistent board member may keep insisting on developing a board policy on some important matter. Maybe the chair or chief executive has resisted board action. Usually, open discussion will resolve this problem, with either the matter being delegated to the staff or the board taking action.

- *Reluctance to challenge.* If the staff is not adhering to a board decision, a board member may question why the board is not willing to hold the chief executive accountable. The board should listen to any modification the chief executive recommends, then make a decision that the chief executive is expected to honor.

- *Lack of monitoring data.* Perhaps the board never defined how to monitor the effectiveness of a particular decision, leaving it subject to interpretation. As a result, some board members think the decision is wrong while others believe it is correct. The solution is to gather solid data so the board knows it already has made a good decision or understands that modifications are needed.

- *Pressure from a donor board member.* A major donor who insists on having his or her way may threaten to stop giving. If the donor's request is in conflict with the organization's mission, the board chair will have a clear answer. In other situations, the board chair must explain the board's rationale for rejecting a donor's request.

PART
4

Good Principles

From time to time, the board should review these decision-making principles:

- Once elected, every board member should think and act for the good of the whole.

- Different points of view should be encouraged at the time an issue is being discussed.

- When everyone feels that the discussion process has been fair and complete, the board chair calls for a vote.

- The majority determines the board's decision, and everyone is obligated to support the decision.

If a board member continually violates these principles, the chair should remind him or her of the duty of loyalty, which obligates board members to act in the best interest of the organization as a whole (see Question 7).

Difficulties arise if a board member takes the disagreement public. Once the board has acted, every board member must fairly represent the will of the board—even if he or she personally disagrees with the decision. Continuing to argue one's minority view outside the board meeting with staff members, donors, or others is out of bounds. Board members must understand that the organization will not tolerate this behavior, and the board must be willing to apply the ultimate sanction—termination of membership—if a board member does not comply.

Divergent opinions on a board are good—but ultimately boards must speak with one voice.

PART
4

SUGGESTED ACTION STEPS

1. Board chair, schedule a ten-minute discussion during a board meeting on the topic of dissenting votes and why they might occur.

2. Board chair and chief executive, if particular board members often oppose legitimate board actions, discuss who should do what, how, and when to address the issue.

45.

How should board minutes be written, approved, and kept?

Minutes from a board meeting are the permanent record that provides information about when the meeting occurred and what action was taken. Minutes are legal documents, but how they must be presented is not defined by law. Some organizations follow strict formats, even adding topical headings or color-coding, while others take a more informal approach.

When establishing or revising your organization's system for taking and maintaining minutes, answer the following questions.

Who should take minutes? In rare instances, the elected board secretary actually takes minutes. More often, a staff member is assigned to the task. That person takes detailed notes and sometimes records the meeting as a backup (although making an audio or video record may present legal concerns as well as hinder an open discussion).

How much detail should be written down? Some attorneys advise writing detailed minutes because they could help should the organization ever go to court. But others maintain that minutes should be brief, recording only formal actions, in case they become part of the discovery process in a lawsuit. Consult your organization's legal counsel for advice.

From the perspective of board members and chief executives, minutes should enable readers to determine easily what decisions were made in the course of the meeting; it is not necessary to explain all the deliberations and discussions behind an action.

What is the best format? Having a consistent format for the minutes makes them easier to write and to read. Begin with the date, place, starting time, board members present, and board members absent. Each page should have a footer indicating the organization name, date, and page number. The narrative should summarize routine opening business and then introduce each item of board business followed by the board decision.

Most board members prefer crisp, clear, accurate minutes that reflect just the facts, not all the dialogue that went into the decisions. In fact, it isn't necessary to record who made, seconded, or amended a motion. The minutes can use shorthand such as "MSC (moved, seconded, and carried): "MSC: Lou Leader be elected chair for one term." Some boards do roll-call votes, with the minutes indicating who voted and how. In some situations, after a chair has declared the results of the vote, a board member may request that "the minutes record that I voted against."

How are minutes approved? After a staff member drafts the minutes, they are circulated for content edits to other staff members who attended the meeting. The draft minutes are then sent to the elected board secretary. The minutes might be signed, "Written by Steve Stickler and approved by Sam Secretary," then mailed to the entire board within two weeks of the meeting. They usually appear again in the advance materials for the next board meeting, at which time they are formally approved, with any amendments, for safekeeping.

Where should minutes be kept? The assistant board secretary or a staff member should store board minutes in files or notebooks in a secure area. The electronic files should also be retained, with a backup set stored offsite.

Some organizations maintain a board reference book that includes minutes of the previous three or four meetings. This portable board library, kept up to date by a staff member, is available at all board meetings. It should include other useful reference documents, such as the bylaws, a list of board members, committee assignments, the previous budget and audit, and a list of staff and programs.

How are committee minutes handled? Executive committee minutes should be kept in a similar fashion and distributed to all board members, who should affirm the committee's decisions at their next meeting. Whether other committees should keep minutes is a matter of choice. Because most committees are only shaping recommendations to the board, minutes are not legally necessary. They are useful for absent committee members, the board chair, or even all board members—but keep them short.

Should minutes be available on the Web? Some board members may want electronic access to the minutes and policies manual by e-mail or the organization's Web site. This information might be made available on an Intranet or a board-members-only section of the Web site accessed by a password. But never deny board members their own hard copies. For boards following the open meeting laws, it may be practical to post the minutes on the organization's Web site for the review of the public.

PART
4

SUGGESTED ACTION STEPS

1. Board members, discuss the format of the minutes and determine which details are necessary to be included.

2. Board chair, be sure the location of the minutes is known. If the task has been neglected, set up a new system in which several people know where to find meeting minutes.

3. Chief executive, if the elected board secretary has been taking minutes, suggest delegating the job to a staff member.

46

How can technology improve board and committee meetings?

Technology holds great potential for streamlining a board's work. The only caution is that state laws govern how nonprofit organizations can make decisions, and states are slow to update their statutes regarding the use of technology.

Following are some examples of how your board might employ technology to enhance productivity and communications during and between meetings.

Face-to-face meetings. Listening to PowerPoint presentations, learning from a video, and taking minutes on a laptop computer are all common features of board meetings. Some organizations with large boards use group decision-making software and electronic polling during their meetings. Others "meet" via videoconference, which can save travel time and expenses for some board members while still allowing them to notice their peers' nonverbal cues and read the tone of speakers' remarks.

Technology can be most useful between live meetings and in committee meetings. Because committees are simply preparing recommendations for board action, few state laws prevent the use of electronic lists for discussion and decision making on routine issues.

Telephone conferences. Boards and committees whose members know one another well might agree that the quality of their decision making won't be compromised significantly by convening meetings via the telephone lines. Although conference calls may reduce the number of in-person meetings, they still require planning, detailed advance materials, a strong chair, and an agreed-upon protocol.

Virtual communities. Your organization can connect with people online no matter where they live. Through online chats, discussion boards, and e-mail forums, you can stay in touch with donors or other constituents who may have moved away from your service area but still want to feel a part of the organization.

Electronic board books. The large mailing envelope, stuffed with minutes, financial reports, and committee updates, is a thing of the past. An e-mail to board members can contain an attachment of all materials relevant to the upcoming meeting—or the organization can establish a board home page on its Web site. Board members download and review the relevant documents on their own schedule.

PART
4

Intranets. These internal, password-protected networks, only for employees or board members, offer an efficient means of communicating information and sharing documents. They can be used to archive minutes or post discussion papers in preparation for the next board meeting, thus cutting down printing and mailing costs. Board members can post messages for one another between meetings.

E-lists. The chair or chief executive can use an e-list to test ideas and options several weeks before a meeting. Having this advance dialogue can lead to improved, shorter discussion at the meeting itself and can be used to solicit feedback from board members who may be unable to attend the meeting. The drawback is that it can become cumbersome, even confusing, to track conversations via e-mail. In addition, comments can be subject to misinterpretation when removed from their face-to-face context because board members are unable to read one another's body language or facial expressions.

Online surveys. Although their statistical validity is sometimes questionable, Web-based surveys can provide snapshots of what constituents are thinking. That input can be helpful when a quick decision is needed.

E-mail newsletters. These short communications—usually no more than four or five paragraphs in length—can keep board and committee members abreast of breaking news in the organization. They may also carry links to content on the organization's Web site.

Online voting. Depending on the state, some board business can be conducted online. Most states, however, have not yet adopted statutes that permit organizations to conduct board elections via the Internet, except maybe in formal membership organizations. If you allow voting electronically, use professional software that ensures accurate and legal rules to be respected. Set up a structured way to verify the person's identity—perhaps through a password—and to ensure that each person votes only once. Only under rare occasions should a self-perpetuating board carry on elections or other voting electronically.

As useful as technology is for governance, heed these cautions:

- Technology is not foolproof. Just when you want to depend on it, it may not work.
- Not everyone is skilled at using the Internet. Be prepared to train board members.
- Some advanced applications are expensive and require staff support.

- Using technology still can turn off some board members.

- Words on the computer screen—in e-mail or chat rooms— often are interpreted differently from the spoken word.

- Privacy is important on some issues. Be wary of hackers, and remind board members not to forward e-mail messages and materials that may contain confidential information intended for their eyes only.

Technology should enhance the process, not replace face-to-face interaction.

SUGGESTED ACTION STEPS

1. Board members, try multiple technologies with one of your committees. Send an e-mail directing them to your Web site for a proposal. Invite committee members to make their comments in a chat-room format for two weeks, and then schedule a telephone conference to reach consensus.

2. Board chair, assign interested board members and staff to a task force that meets with experts and reports to the board on potential uses of technology.

PART
4

PART FIVE

The Board's Role as a Fiduciary

By definition, a fiduciary is someone who has a special trust or responsibility to fulfill certain obligations to others. In a nonprofit organization, those obligations encompass both the legal and financial realms. Entrusted with guarding the organization's assets and reputation, board members must make prudent decisions that are in the best interest of the organization, without subjecting it to unnecessary risk.

As a board member, you are also a steward of the organization's mission, as well as the public's trust. A board member's oversight role entails setting and maintaining high standards of financial accountability; establishing and adhering to guidelines for ethical and legal behavior; and operating in a transparent manner so that contributors, members, constituents, and other stakeholders understand how and why critical decisions were made.

Note: Information presented in this section is not intended as a substitute for legal advice. For the latest details on legal developments, including state and federal laws regarding nonprofit organizations, consult an attorney with expertise in those areas.

47.

How does a board help ensure the organization's long-term viability?

The road to long-term financial viability is different for every organization. Reaching this goal depends on the type and age of the organization, its values, the nature of the competition, leadership, and much more. Some nonprofits are successful risk takers, while others take a conservative approach to finances and build their net reserves each year. Some organizations may focus on building endowments, while others may place a higher priority on meeting programming demands.

Long-term financial viability is less a strategy and more the outcome of hundreds of good practices and wise decisions over time. Boards looking ahead to the financial future should focus on these areas:

- A *clear, well-communicated mission and goals.* No one wants to give money to organizations whose purpose is unclear or whose successes are not well known. Staying clear on the organization's mission and major goals also helps a board focus on which revenues and expenses are most appropriate. Chasing after new revenue sources just for the sake of the bottom line may dilute the organization's mission and end up alienating dues-paying members, donors, and other supporters.

- *Financial discipline and transparency.* More and more, major donors as well as dues-paying members want to know the nitty gritty details about how money is made and spent, what financial controls are in place, what policies govern financial management, and how finances are monitored. The board must be willing and able to share this information with donors and supporters.

- *Multiple revenue sources.* Depending on one or two activities or funders to provide the majority of annual revenue can result in a financial crisis when even one source dries up.

Although some boards think membership dues will always amount to 90 percent of revenues, a membership base creates all kinds of opportunities for providing a service and generating new revenue streams at the same time. Some charities have always depended on mail solicitation, but major donor giving—including deferred giving through a planned giving program—makes mass mailings a poor strategy for organizations whose mission is directed toward a small group of people or organizations.

PART 5

Potential Sources of Income

Many nonprofits have found entrepreneurial ways to generate enough earned income that contributed income becomes a pool of extra money for special projects (see Question 56). The challenge is to match the mission to the money.

How many possible ways to generate income does your organization tap? Creativity and alliances with other organizations are necessary for most nonprofit corporations today. Some of the options in Exhibit 47.1 require business partnerships, risk taking, and

EXHIBIT 47.1. Methods of Income Generation.

Revenues and Reimbursements
Memberships
Tuition and registration fees
Sales of products and services
Subscriptions
Contracts to provide services
Insurance and other reimbursements
Other

Contributions

	Individuals (current and deferred giving)	Government	Business	Foundations	Nonprofit Organizations
Annual giving	X		X		X
Mass appeal	X				
Program or operational grants	X	X	X	X	X
Events	X		X		
Capital funds	X		X	X	X
In-kind	X		X		X

Investment Income

	Organization	For-Profit Subsidiary
Cash and fixed income accounts	X	
Securities	X	
Real estate rental	X	
Real estate development/sales	X	
Dividends from subsidiary		X
Sale of subsidiary		X
Other	X	X

Source: The ideas for these categories were inspired by *The Board Member's Guide to Fund Raising* by Fisher Howe (Jossey-Bass, 1991).

legal and tax challenges, but others could be natural, low-risk extensions of what you are already doing.

SUGGESTED ACTION STEPS

1. Board chair, ask the chief executive to develop a chart showing the sources of revenue for your organization over the past ten years and to identify how sources have shifted.

2. Board members, create benchmarks to measure your financial strength.

3. Board chair, periodically invite financial advisers to educate the board on financial trends in the nonprofit sector. Make sure the speaker can translate financial terms and jargon into plain English and is open to answering questions.

48.

What does the board need to know about reserves and investments?

Reserves, also referred to as the fund balance, is what remains after the organization's financial obligations, as defined by the budget, are subtracted from the organization's assets. Think of your organization's reserves as a "rainy day" fund—a means of cushioning unexpected shifts in the economy, enduring dramatic changes in donations or the loss of a major revenue source, or providing the means to invest in a new or unexpected opportunity.

Nonprofit organizations generally are advised to maintain reserves equal to between three and six months of their annual operating budget. In other words, an organization with a $900,000 annual budget ideally would have reserves of $450,000 in case a cash-flow emergency were to arise. An organization planning to buy a building may accumulate much more extensive reserves, only to see the fund decrease dramatically after the purchase takes place. Still others, such as educational institutions, build and maintain a high level of reserves to ensure generational equity—a means of providing support far into the future, for many years to come.

Some stakeholders may take issue with earmarking money for reserves when it could be spent delivering the programs and services that remain the organization's reason for being. Indeed, generational equity is not usually an issue for organizations focused on the here and now, such as disaster relief groups that respond to an immediate, specific crisis. Depending on mission, financial philosophy, and donors' attitudes, the board should set a goal for the amount of unrestricted reserves and when to tap into it. This is known as the reserve policy.

The board, guided by the finance committee and with an eye on the strategic plan, must balance short- and long-term objectives when crafting or revising the reserve policy. For instance, a higher level of reserves may be warranted if the organization is contemplating new program initiatives (which carry higher financial risk) or a major purchase.

You might hear the phrase "liquid reserves," or operating reserve. This refers to cash on hand and assets that can easily be converted to cash with little risk of loss (such as marketable securities). In contrast, "non-liquid reserves" refer to the headquarters office and those assets tied up in furniture, equipment, other property, a for-profit subsidiary, or a related foundation. Converting them into cash not only takes longer but also carries a higher risk of loss.

Investment Guidelines

Liquid reserves represent the funds available for *investments*. The reserve policy set by the board, taken together with the organization's cash flow, will guide the type of investments selected. Most organizations have an operational cycle with high points and low points for revenue—a certain month or time of year when charitable contributions are received, a large program takes place, or dues are collected. If the organization's balance drops to zero right before the expected influx of revenue, the organization would need to quickly generate cash. That would point to the need for short-term, low-risk investments such as Treasury bills and insured certificates of deposit.

Even the cash needed to cover day-to-day operations can be invested in some way, such as earning interest on a checking account and not paying invoices until they are due.

Some organizations maintain a sweep account that's equivalent to two or three weeks of day-to-day operations. The organization earns investment income on the account and has access to it each day; whatever is not spent is automatically reinvested.

In general, investment guidelines generally cover the following elements:

- *The organization's overall investment philosophy.* This guides decisions for the long term, making organizations more likely to stay the course during turbulent economic times rather than to panic and pull out all assets. An organization, for instance, might abide by a 60:40 philosophy, such as having 60 percent in equities (mostly value stocks) and 40 percent in fixed assets.

- *The kinds of investments allowed or prohibited.* Each option involves a different degree of risk, investment yield, and ability to access the funds (liquidity). In general, the lower the risk, the greater the liquidity (think of a savings account that pays low interest but allows for withdrawal of funds at any time). An investment vehicle promising a higher yield also carries a higher risk (junk bonds, for example).

  Most nonprofit organizations take a conservative approach and aim for a mix of low-risk, short-term investments (those that mature within one to five years, such as mutual funds) and higher-risk, long-term investments (stocks and bonds held for more than five years). Some nonprofits are more aggressive and have adopted policies that allow them to invest in hedge funds and venture-capital deals. Some are

concerned with socially responsible investing. Thus they
avoid supporting tobacco companies or corporations that
use child labor, for example, or choose to support those companies that engage in environmentally safe activities.

- *How investments should be allocated.* What percentage should
  stocks represent? What percentage should be in bonds? The
  guidelines should provide the rationale for each class of assets
  selected and explain how, taken together, they offer balance
  and diversity.

- *How performance will be measured.* At a minimum, investment yield should be reviewed quarterly. Decide what index
  to use as a performance benchmark, such as the Standard &
  Poor's 500.

- *How often, and in what format, the full board will receive reports.*

If the size and diversity of your investments merit it, appoint an
investment committee to handle much of the detailed analysis of investment choices and make recommendations for the board to review
and approve. With members well-versed in money management, the
investment committee can come up with policies and a strategy that
meet the organization's current needs while reflecting economic
trends such as inflation, consumer spending, and interest rates. These
guidelines would be forwarded to the board for approval.

Incidentally, the investment committee is one place where you
don't want to see a lot of turnover from one year to the next. People
need time to understand the organization's investment strategy and
financial culture. For continuity and a commitment to long-term
results, add only one new member every two years or so. Just guard
against keeping the same membership in place for so long that iner-
tia sets in. The organization's investment philosophy and policies
must be revisited frequently and revised to accommodate economic
fluctuations as well as changes or developments in mission-related
activities.

Note that neither members of the investment committee nor members of the board select particular stocks or mutual funds or otherwise manage the organization's investments. Their job is to set investment guidelines and monitor investment performance.

SUGGESTED ACTION STEPS

1. Board chair, ask your auditor to provide data on the reserve policies of similar nonprofits within the community.

2. Board chair, invite a representative from the investment committee or your investment management firm to update board members on the organization's current investment philosophy.

3. Board chair, work with an outside investment adviser who has experience in the nonprofit sector, to avoid having board members manage the organization's investments.

PART
5

Q A

49.

What is the board's role in the budget?

The annual operating budget outlines the organization's goals and activities for the year and attaches numbers. The document estimates income from a variety of sources and sets forth the organization's anticipated expenditures for the year. Staff members have the responsibility for determining which items are covered in the budget and for drafting the overall document. It is the board's responsibility to review and approve the budget, after making sure it accurately reflects the organization's mission.

Some members who are new to the board may express surprise that the budget calls for a surplus rather than breaking even, as the term "nonprofit" may suggest. A board-level discussion might be in order, with the board chair or other leaders noting that nonprofits have the main goal of advancing a charitable, social, professional, humanitarian, or educational cause. Yet although nonprofits are not primarily in business to make a profit, they are not prohibited from doing so. In fact, under most circumstances, building a surplus constitutes a wise business practice.

A nonprofit reinvests its profits in programs and operations that advance its mission, instead of paying profits to shareholders in the form of cash dividends as for-profits do. An end-of-the-year surplus for a nonprofit not only points to successful efforts by both staff and volunteers but also gives the organization something to invest for those years when the balance sheet tips the other way.

Among the budget-related questions to ask are the following:

- *Does the board regularly receive financial statements that include budget information?* It's helpful for board members to compare actual expenses and revenues to those budgeted, including the percentage of variance. These statements should be reviewed regularly during board meetings so that all board members remain aware of profit-and-loss performance.

- *Who develops the budget each year?* If board members have a role in budget development (in organizations without the appropriate staff), they must have access to the information needed to make realistic projections (such as prior-year performance or pricing trends within the field).

- *Where are revenues projected to come from?* The financial markets are too fickle to rely on investment returns as part of specific projected revenues, unless the organization has money market or certificates of deposit accounts exclusively. Warning bells should sound if the proposed operating budget relies heavily on income from investment portfolios that contain equity holdings. (The exception would be a foundation that typically spends a set percentage of its net investment assets each year.)

- *What are the operating ratios for key areas?* Determine what percentage of total budgeted expenditures goes to such areas as salaries and benefits, fundraising, publishing, and so forth. Some donors may request such information to determine, for example, how much of every dollar raised goes directly to support programs or services.

PART 5

- *What policies apply to budget revisions?* How much flexibility does the staff have to reallocate income or expenses as the fiscal year unfolds? For example, mid-year adjustments are common and considered normal in many organizations. Requiring board approval on any significant revisions can be an effective internal control: fraudulent activity or misuse of funds may come to light. In addition, if a program does not meet revenue expectations and a shortfall is likely, the board can swiftly take corrective action, such as scaling back other programs or postponing some expenditures.

- *How do the organization's revenues and expenditures stack up against those of other nonprofits?* To make well-informed financial decisions, board members also need to remain abreast of trends within the community and the nonprofit sector as a whole. Helpful benchmarks may include membership or donor retention rates, cost to acquire a new donor or member, average program or product costs, and what percentage of each dollar raised goes to program delivery versus administrative costs.

SUGGESTED ACTION STEPS

1. Board chair, periodically devote part of a board meeting to financial education; ask outside experts or board members serving on the finance committee to review financial policies and budgetary procedures.

2. Board members, compare your operating ratios to those of similar organizations to get a better picture of how well you're doing (or what you could be doing better).

PART
5

50.

What is the board's role in the annual financial audit?

In 2002, primarily in response to financial scandals at several major corporations, the U.S. Congress passed the Sarbanes-Oxley Act. It includes auditing requirements, such as the need to use a different individual auditor at least every five years, for publicly traded companies. Although Sarbanes-Oxley applies primarily to the for-profit sector (except for two clauses), many nonprofit organizations have voluntarily adopted the requirements as being the best practices to follow. Several states have already moved beyond allowing self-regulation and have considered or passed legislation based on Sarbanes-Oxley that affect the nonprofit sector.

Regardless of your state's legal requirements, most organizations would no doubt benefit from an annual audit of their financial activities, conducted by an independent auditing firm. Doing so would reflect the board's commitment to independent assessment of the accuracy of the organization's financial health.

An annual external financial audit, conducted by a competent firm, assures board members that the organization's financial systems and safeguards are appropriate. It helps board members fulfill their fiduciary responsibilities by verifying that accounting standards; federal, state, and local laws; Internal Revenue Service (IRS) regulations; and government grant restrictions are being followed. It reduces the risk that the IRS may impose intermediate sanctions— otherwise known as fines—for improper financial transactions (see Question 7). In addition, an audit provides donors with evidence of sound financial practices, so they know that their contributions are being used wisely.

Use the following suggestions to make sure your organization receives the most benefit from its next annual audit.

- *Delegate responsibility to a committee.* The audit committee acts on behalf of the board and keeps the board apprised of its concerns and recommendations. Committee members should include at least one financial expert who is familiar with non-profit finances and accounting. Although the staff works most closely with the auditor, the board must assume responsibility for defining the scope of work and addressing any suggestions included in the management letter from the auditor.

- *Outline expectations.* The basic audit package will include internal accounting practices, controls, financial management, and financial reports. If requested, some firms will also prepare the IRS Form 990 (see Question 54). Working with the chief financial officer, the committee should describe its expectations beyond those basic components. For example, you might want to evaluate the accounting practices of your regional sites or focus on how accounts payable are handled.

- *Solicit proposals.* The committee should then ask for proposals from two or three audit firms with experience in the nonprofit sector. Better yet, look for firms that have audited similar organizations or that have proven experience with your particular needs. Although there are advantages to working with the same firm each year, it's wise to change audit firms periodically to ensure objectivity.

- *Review the proposals, conduct interviews, and recommend a firm.* This step will give the committee confidence in the firm it recommends to the board. Audit costs can vary from a few thousand dollars to tens of thousands, depending on the size and complexity of the organization's financial structure, so the value received is worth analyzing.

- *Conduct the audit.* Staff members usually assist with the audit, which begins shortly after the end of the fiscal year as soon as the records are organized. Typically, one or two accountants visit the headquarters site to examine financial records and interview staff. The board is unlikely to be involved at this stage.

- *Review a draft report and management letter.* If possible, the audit firm should prepare a draft report and management letter for the chief financial officer and staff. This review often prompts new questions or signals to the audit firm that they overlooked something important. The chief financial officer may be asked to provide a written response to the draft.

- *Distribute the final audit report to the audit or finance committee.* After reading the audit report and management letter carefully, the committee should invite the auditors to discuss their findings. This is the time to ask the auditors about any special concerns and to understand any recommendations, often contained in a separate management letter.

PART
5

Ideally, after reviewing the audit, the full board should meet with the auditor in an executive session. This allows the board the comfort to ask questions that might be delicate in front of the staff.

What if your organization cannot afford a full audit or believes that its finances are too limited to justify one? If the organization is still in its first year or two of operation, without a lot of financial history, it probably does not yet need an audit. In addition, small organizations whose budgets would be taxed by the costs of a full independent audit might wait a few years—provided the board ensures that sound financial policies and reporting procedures are already in place and being followed.

To fulfill the board's fiduciary responsibility to the public, some external oversight is essential. At a minimum, the board should ask an independent certified public accountant to review the staff's accounting and reporting procedures. A small nonprofit should also consider conducting an audit every two or three years.

SUGGESTED ACTION STEPS

1. Board chair, if your organization does not engage an independent audit firm every year or every other year, ask a few board members to investigate your options and report back.

2. Board chair, add value to your audit firm's services by asking the assigned board committee to brainstorm with staff members about the specific issues next year's audit should include.

51.

What should we do if the finances seem amiss?

Any nonprofit, large or small, can be the target of illegal financial activity such as fraud. Anyone with access to financial transactions, from order-processing clerks to the chief executive to the treasurer, can capitalize on opportunities to move money from the organization's coffers into his or her own pockets. Smaller-scale fraud—say, losses of $10,000 or even $100,000—may not make a splash on the evening news, but it can be financially and emotionally devastating to a nonprofit that counts every penny and values its reputation.

"I can't believe it!" is what most people say when they learn an employee or board member has been stealing equipment or supplies, forging checks, perpetrating credit card fraud, or otherwise embezzling from a nonprofit. Unfortunately, it happens.

The temptation may be to handle the situation internally and quietly ask for repayment and the employee's resignation. After all, once the media gets wind of financial malfeasance, your organization is sure to be front-page news, and the resulting coverage could affect financial and volunteer support. But you must report the crime to the proper authorities. Just put yourself in the position of hiring a new chief executive: Wouldn't you want to know if that person had a history of fraud or embezzlement? If you allow the chief executive to depart without a proper investigation, he or she may victimize another nonprofit in the future.

Appropriate Oversight

Instituting internal controls is part of risk management. Having controls in place lessens or eliminates opportunities for fraudulent activity. To minimize the potential for employee theft, a nonprofit board can put appropriate safeguards in place, such as those described as follows.

Emphasize the board's role as financial monitor. As part of new board member orientation, review the position's fiduciary responsibilities (see Question 8). The board's accountability goes beyond telling the chief executive to make sure everything gets done. All board members should understand and feel comfortable with the accounting method used (cash versus accrual), statement of financial position (assets and liabilities), statement of activities (actual receipts and expenditures, usually compared with the budgeted amounts), and cash flow statement (which resources are available at a certain time). Your organization may also develop a capital expenditure budget to cover long-term assets that can be depreciated.

Delegate in-depth financial reviews to high-level committees. Unless board members have a financial background, their eyes are likely to glaze over when they're presented with page upon page of numbers. To keep the board focused on the organization's overall financial picture, have the finance committee review monthly and quarterly reports, the annual budget, the annual audit, and financial policies before their presentation to the board (see Question 15). Other responsibilities may include recommending an auditing firm and ensuring that the organization meets its regulatory requirements. The treasurer serves as the committee's liaison to the board of directors.

Some organizations have a separate investment committee that, in consultation with the finance committee, looks at short- and long-term opportunities for growth. It's crucial that the committees reach beyond the board of directors for their members, ideally tapping volunteers who are bankers, accountants, or money managers. Regardless of their expertise, finance-related committees should forward recommendations to the board for approval, so that the final decision and responsibility ultimately rest with the elected leadership.

Institute checks and balances. Although you don't want board members involved in day-to-day operations, such as signing all checks prepared by the staff, implement policies to govern large transactions or decisions with financial implications. For instance, you might require the chief executive and board chair to cosign checks over the amount of $10,000. Transferring funds from one account to another may require the approval of one or two executive committee members. A member of the executive or finance committee might have the responsibility of meeting with the chief executive and the auditor to review the firm's findings and specific recommendations, without other employees present.

Ultimately, the full board should meet with the auditor and be able to ask questions directly. This practice enforces the sense of fiduciary duty that each board member needs to embrace.

Internal systems should also include fraud controls. For example, the person who opens the envelopes containing charitable contributions should not be the same person who records the contributions or deposits them in the bank. Whoever signs the checks should not also balance the bank statement each month. Although such procedures may seem cumbersome, especially in a nonprofit with a small staff, they can reduce temptation for would-be embezzlers.

Establish human resources policies. Managers in charge of hiring should be required to check employment references and credentials.

PART
5

Employees who commit fraud rely on lies, so when applying for a new job they are likely to submit a resume with fictitious employment or achievements. Human resources personnel should trust their intuition if they are uncomfortable with someone's explanation of a gap in employment or educational credentials. A few phone calls might uncover a pattern of deception.

Also, every employee who comes in contact with money, including part-time and temporary hires, should be bonded.

Your auditor may have additional fraud-prevention suggestions tailored to fit your organization's size, structure, and type of operations. As an objective outsider, the auditor can more clearly identify areas in which employees, suppliers, or volunteers could easily engage in wrongdoing. Just don't rely solely on your auditor to detect fraud. Although auditors do spotchecks of selected statements and documents as part of the annual audit, they are not necessarily looking for fraudulent activity. In addition, they work from the documents and explanations provided by staff members who may have something to hide.

Suspicious Activity

Several behaviors may point to fraudulent activity. Be on the lookout for an employee who

- Continually hires and fires other employees, especially those with access to financial records
- Often mentions being behind on work and needing to stay late or come in on weekends to catch up
- Has difficulty producing financial reports on schedule or responding to requests for receipts or account statements
- Insists on personally handling certain tasks because "No one else could figure out my system"
- Always meets with the auditors alone; discourages others from talking with auditors

- Appears to have financial problems, perhaps related to drug or alcohol abuse or gambling debts
- Gets caught in little white lies
- Doesn't take vacations
- Acquires an expensive habit or makes an extravagant purchase that seems beyond his or her means and openly talks about it

If you and other board members suspect fraud within your organization, or if an employee has raised the subject with you, quietly gather evidence. Look for altered documents, conflicting financial statements, payments to companies the organization does not do business with, and so forth. Should the evidence point to a long-standing pattern of deceit, arrange for a forensic audit that looks back several years.

Guard against making any public statements that could be construed as slander. If your assumptions prove incorrect or if you need more time to gather evidence, your statements could put you at legal risk.

Assuming you have evidence of wrongdoing in hand, call local law enforcement officials to report the crime and stop the thief in his or her tracks. The chief executive should handle this if the fraud involves another employee; the board chair should make the call if the chief executive is suspected. If the crime violates federal laws, the Federal Bureau of Investigation may become involved as well.

PART
5

SUGGESTED ACTION STEPS

1. Board chair, arrange for the full board to meet with the auditor, without staff present, to review internal controls and identify any areas in which controls are lacking.

2. Board members, develop a whistleblower policy—a process through which employees can report suspected fraud without fear of reprisal.

52.

What conflict-of-interest policies should we adopt?

The professional expertise and personal contacts a board member brings to a nonprofit organization can be invaluable. For example, introductions from a board member can open doors to new sources of funding or to more cost-effective suppliers. Committed board members are always on the lookout for ways they can help the organization.

Certainly, ethical violations or other improprieties are hardly, if ever, on the minds of those who agree to serve an organization that is dedicated to doing charitable, educational, or humanitarian work. But busy individuals have numerous interests and may be engaged in activities that create conflicts of priority. A board member has a duty of loyalty to the organization on whose board he or she serves. When personal interests collide with organizational interests, they need to be managed appropriately.

These kinds of activities may involve—but aren't limited to—financial dealings. Wanting the organization to save some of its precious dollars, for example, a board member may offer his or her legal expertise to draft contracts or agreements. The board chair may capitalize on the position's high profile and be named to the board of a funding agency to keep an eye out for the organization. An employee may suggest channeling business to a startup firm, which happens to be owned by a family member. Or the organization may make a large purchase from a company owned by a board member.

If due diligence is not part of hiring processes, vendor choices, or the signing of any contracts, the nonprofit risks losing its good reputation, and the board members may appear to fail to meet the legal standard of putting the organization first before their own personal gain. Lapses in ethical or moral behavior can instantly attract media attention and draw the ire of the community: when people "on the inside" profit from a nonprofit's activities, this may lead to private inurement or personal benefit. The public's trust is violated, and the organization's nonprofit status may be put in jeopardy.

Recommended Practices

Conflicts of interest, sometimes referred to as duality of interest, happen all the time. In fact, they're inevitable. But they are also manageable. Following are practices to help avoid any appearance of impropriety, which can be as damaging as an actual occurrence of it.

Conflicts-of-interest policy. Start with a written policy for both board and staff that outlines standards of conduct that reflect personal and organizational integrity. This policy should require full disclosure of a board member's connections with any individuals, groups, and companies doing business with the organization. The majority of nonprofit organizations surveyed by BoardSource—75 percent—have a conflict-of-interest policy, and 57 percent of them have referred to the policy in the preceding two years.

In the document, provide examples of actual and perceived conflicts of interest—specific instances when a board member might find it difficult to make an objective decision. An awareness of what potentially constitutes a conflict of interest and subtle reminders of

PART
5

board members' obligations can keep everyone focused on what's best for the organization.

Disclosure statement. Work with legal counsel to develop a statement for each board member to sign that identifies, or discloses, potential conflicts of interest. In signing this disclosure statement, typically once a year, board members also signify their understanding of and agreement with the standards of conduct. Assure board members that the statements will remain confidential and would be disclosed only to an attorney or auditor should a serious problem arise. The statement, in a nonthreatening manner, should ask the board member to

- Disclose personal or professional affiliations (including those of immediate family members) with companies the nonprofit organization does business with. Board members should report, for instance, whether they hold a sizable amount of stock or have other financial interests in a company.
- Disclose any personal business dealings (including those of immediate family members) he or she has had with the nonprofit organization in the previous twelve months.
- List other corporate or nonprofit boards on which he or she (or an immediate family member) serves. This helps reveal whether a board member may be put in the position to raise funds for competing organizations or handle confidential information in an inappropriate manner.

Policy review with new members. When recruiting new board members, identify conflicts of interest that may arise and explain the disclosure policy they will be asked to sign. If a major conflict of interest seems likely to arise during his or her term in office, you may want to postpone that person's election to the board.

Guidelines for handling potential conflict. Develop guidelines for identifying potential conflicts of interest among both board and staff and for handling any situation that arises. Following are some examples:

- Before voting on an agenda item related to an expenditure or the awarding of a contract, the board chair should ask all directors whether a real or potential conflict of interest exists.

- When a conflict of interest has been identified, the board member should excuse himself or herself from the discussion and the decision. The board chair may need to issue a reminder for the board member to leave the room.

- If a conflict of interest comes to the attention of the organization, designate who will discuss it with the board member involved (for example, the board chair or the executive committee). Include a provision for addressing conflicts of interest that involve the board chair.

- Establish procedures for obtaining competitive bids on outsourced jobs. For instance, require that every job costing $1,000 or more be put out for bid to at least three vendors. This step shows that employees have conducted cost-comparison research and provides supporting documentation if the contract is ultimately awarded to someone having ties to the organization.

- Ask staff members to update their conflict-of-interest forms annually. These forms should be similar to those signed by the board of directors.

- Prohibit staff members from serving on the board of directors, which sets policies and makes financial decisions that affect their livelihood (see Question 67). One exception is the chief executive, who often is designated as an ex officio and often nonvoting member of the board (see Question 61).

- Prohibit staff members from devoting time on the job or using office equipment to pursue projects for personal gain, whether financial or professional. If an employee writes a book, operates a business, or runs for public office, for instance, he or she

PART
5

must do it outside the workplace to avoid any appearance of impropriety.

Ultimately, an organization must trust its judgment in selecting board members on whom it can depend to do the right thing: be loyal to the organization and promote its best interests rather than their own personal agendas. Few conflicts of interest in themselves are illegal; they simply need proper attention and handling.

SUGGESTED ACTION STEPS

1. Board members, establish board guidelines for identifying and handling potential conflicts of interest; communicate these to incoming board members.

2. Board members, develop a statement of full disclosure for each board and senior staff member to review and sign annually.

Q&A 53.

How can we protect the organization—and ourselves— from lawsuits?

The legal aspects of serving on a nonprofit board may surprise some board members who see the position as an honorary one or as recognition of community or professional achievements. In fact, board officers and directors may be named in lawsuits filed against the organization because they remain accountable for the organization's actions. Ignorance of illegal activity is not an adequate defense.

Numerous protections—some minimal and some substantial— exist for board members. If a nonprofit is incorporated, for instance, state laws may limit the personal liability for officers and directors who are unpaid volunteers and who do not engage in willful or reckless conduct. At the federal level, the Volunteer Protection Act protects unpaid volunteers acting within the scope of their organizational responsibilities at the time, provided their actions do not lead to criminal misconduct or gross negligence.

The Volunteer Protection Act does not prevent volunteers from being named in lawsuits, nor does it protect them from civil rights violations (such as discrimination) and sexual harassment offenses. Also, it does not protect the organization itself, which can still be held liable for the actions of its volunteers.

To further shelter volunteers from personal liability arising from legal actions, numerous nonprofit organizations indemnify board members—if the state laws allow it—usually through a resolution or bylaws provision. Depending on the state's laws, indemnification may allow the organization to reimburse a volunteer for legal expenses incurred or to pay the cost of any damages assessed, unless fraud, gross negligence, or criminal activity occurred.

Of course, indemnification is meaningless if the organization doesn't have sufficient funds or assets to cover the costs of legal actions against its volunteers. That's why most organizations purchase directors and officers (D&O) liability insurance. This coverage is in addition to the organization's comprehensive general liability policy, which covers claims related to property damage, theft, and bodily injury. According to BoardSource research, 87 percent of responding organizations carry D&O insurance.

D&O insurance protects against harm resulting from decisions made by the board, including employment practices, mismanagement of finances, and antitrust violations. Depending on the policy, it might cover attorney's fees, fines, penalties, or punitive damages. In most states, however, D&O insurance does not cover civil fines, such as those assessed by the Internal Revenue Service. Other exclusions might include claims of libel, slander, antitrust violations, and sexual harassment. In addition, coverage may be denied if the organization fails to give notice of a claim to the insurance company within a specified period of time.

Six Areas to Watch

Establishing and enforcing internal controls, in the form of clearly stated policies, is the best form of protection against legal action. A board can reduce its risk by establishing and periodically reviewing policies and procedures related to the six key areas described as follows.

Employment. Legal experts report that the majority of lawsuits filed against nonprofit organizations pertain to personnel issues. These cases run the gamut from discriminatory hiring to wrongful termination, from sexual harassment to breach of contract. Recommended practices include the following:

- Ensure that anyone in a position to hire or terminate employees understands and complies with state and federal laws. These usually relate to employment interviews and procedures for termination.

- Develop position descriptions that clearly spell out the job-related qualifications and performance criteria.

- Conduct thorough reference and criminal background checks on potential employees.

- Follow a formal process for conducting annual performance reviews, including a written plan agreed to by the employee and manager, for improving skills or competencies.

- Draft a grievance policy that provides a means for employees to report fraudulent, discriminatory, or harassing behavior without fear of reprisal. An employee who believes that the chief executive is engaging in unethical activity, for example, should be able to freely report the situation to someone else in the organization.

- Establish a process for handling potential disputes, such as calling in a third-party investigator, a mediator, or an arbitrator. Taking steps toward alternative dispute resolution may lead to a compromise and keep the issue out of the legal system.

- Have legal counsel regularly review employment applications and personnel handbooks to ensure that they comply with recent developments in employment law.

Governance. Each board member needs to be aware of the legal obligations that come with board service. The duties of care, loyalty, and obedience define the expectations for individual board members as they fulfill their governance role (see Question 7).

Attend meetings, come prepared, and pose questions when you do not understand something. Ensure that the mission of the organization is the primary motivator when making decisions. Familiarize yourself with the laws that govern nonprofits. Be sure to brief board and staff members on the potential for conflicts of interest and ask them to sign annual disclosure statements (see Question 52).

Financial Activity. A board may choose to assign some duties to a finance committee, such as reviewing the budgets prepared by the staff, but it remains accountable for the organization's financial health. The board's best defense against a claim is being able to show, through meeting minutes and other documentation, that it exerted appropriate oversight.

With the assistance of an external auditor, ensure that appropriate internal controls exist to oversee financial transactions, approve or authorize major expenditures, safeguard assets from risk, and comply with state and federal reporting requirements. Set guidelines for potential reimbursement of travel expenses and the use of a corporate credit card or charge account. In addition, have a policy detailing how any financial discrepancies will be investigated (see Question 51).

Business Operations. Develop written contracts for big-ticket items or services purchased from suppliers or contractors. Although some contracts can exist between two parties without being put in writing, you're more likely to remember all the tasks and details involved when obligated to record them.

Ensure that contracts include standard language and provisions, such as appropriate use of trademarks, terms of payment, a cancellation clause, and a mechanism for dispute resolution. Ask your attorney to review any contracts that involve large expenditures, and don't hesitate to propose changes to contracts supplied by vendors.

Fundraising. It's helpful to have policies that outline what type of gifts and grants the organization will accept and the extent of due diligence required before a decision is made. For instance, define acceptable conditional or restricted gifts (to be spent only as specified by the donor) or clarify under what conditions the organization will accept gifts of buildings or land. What about federal grant money? Receiving federal grants generally requires a nonprofit to provide reports that may prove cumbersome for a small staff to produce; if those reports are incomplete or aren't filed on a timely basis the grant could be in jeopardy.

Volunteers. Double-check that your general liability insurance covers injuries that volunteers, employees, or other visitors may sustain while attending an event sponsored by the organization or held at its facilities. Also, to reduce the likelihood of discrimination claims, have standardized procedures in place for recruiting and terminating volunteers.

Personal Liability Checklist

Just to be on the safe side, board members should do the following to minimize the risks of board service:

- Always act in the best interest of the organization.
- Disclose any potential conflicts of interest.
- Review the monthly and quarterly financial reports, and read the auditor's annual report.
- Do your homework before voting on an issue; thoroughly review background materials, especially any legal or financial documents.

- Take time to deliberate before casting a vote; ask thoughtful questions, and don't allow yourself to be rushed into a decision.
- Ensure that the meeting minutes reflect any dissenting votes.

When the chief executive and board of directors abide by a code of conduct and work together to develop comprehensive policies and procedures, the organization has a good chance of limiting potential liability for all parties. Purchasing D&O insurance coverage provides the organization with added protection and gives key volunteers peace of mind as they fulfill their fiduciary and governance responsibilities.

SUGGESTED ACTION STEPS

1. Chief executive, conduct a risk management and legal audit to ensure that your board and staff have policies in all applicable areas.
2. Board chair, review with board members the scope of the Volunteer Protection Act and your organization's indemnification policies.
3. Board members, periodically review your organization's directors and officers (D&O) insurance policy.

PART
5

Q&A

54.

What is a Form 990?

Each year, the Internal Revenue Service (IRS) requires a nonprofit with more than $25,000 in annual revenue to file Form 990 (Return of Organization Exempt from Income Tax). This annual report of revenue, expenses, assets, liabilities, and income-producing activities is due five months after the close of the organization's fiscal year, on the 15th of that month. If, for example, the fiscal year ends on December 31, Form 990 must be filed by May 15 of the following calendar year.

Often a certified public accountant prepares Form 990. It is the board's responsibility, however, to ensure that this happens. Otherwise, the organization may have to pay a penalty based on every day the tax return is late if no extension for filing was granted.

The IRS may also assess penalties on an organization that does not make its three most recent filings of Form 990 available for public inspection. By law, an organization must comply immediately with any in-person request to review its Form 990 during normal business hours. Alternatively, an organization has thirty days in which to comply with a written request (letter, fax, or e-mail) and may charge a reasonable fee to cover copying and postage costs.

According to the IRS (www.irs.gov), an organization does not have to fulfill individual requests if it makes its tax returns widely available, such as posting the forms on its own Web site or on an on-line database of nonprofits such as GuideStar (www.guidestar.org). The names and addresses of contributors to the organization (unless it is a private foundation) are withheld from public disclosure.

Although Form 990 is a legal document, it can also serve as a detailed introduction to your organization for anyone wishing to know more about its mission, functions, and funding. In fact, Form 990 can be an effective public relations tool because it is freely available to the press, potential funders, and the general public. So make sure it is accurate and that it represents the organization and its activities in a truthful manner.

The form itself has a limited amount of space, but attachments are unlimited; that enables the organization to attach background information, such as program-related brochures, that expand upon the cut-and-dry financial descriptions. Form 990 also reports the names and compensation of the five highest-paid staff members. Providing these additional details not only underscores what the organization is all about but also positions it as one that operates transparently.

In addition, most states require nonprofit organizations to register annually if they carry on fundraising or other business activities within the state.

PART
5

SUGGESTED ACTION STEPS

1. Chief executive, review the filing schedule for state and federal financial reports, to ensure that all deadlines are met.

2. Board members, look at the organization's Form 990 as posted on its Web site or on a database of nonprofits. Discuss additional information that could be attached to the form to present the organization in the best possible light.

55.

Does every board member have to make a personal gift?

By serving on the board, you publicly show your support of the organization's mission, vision, and values. It's only natural that your belief in that good work should translate into a personal contribution to an annual giving program and, when applicable, to a capital campaign. After all, one of your responsibilities as a board member is to ensure that the organization prospers financially—and you personally can help make that happen by making a personal gift.

The board should have a policy to guide personal giving by board members; at a minimum, it should explain that every board member is expected to make an annual contribution to the organization. The policy should emphasize that each board member should consider the organization as his or her priority for charitable giving and that the personal gift should be a meaningful or "stretch" amount for each individual.

It usually is best not to state a specific amount in the policy. Doing so could backfire. Say, for example, a policy calls for each board member to contribute $2,000 annually. The organization may be losing or scaring away board members who do not have those financial resources but have other valuable talents or skills to contribute. In addition, such a policy might actually diminish contributions; a board member might be prepared to write a check for $5,000 but understands that only $2,000 is expected.

Some high-status boards have the clout within a community to make board membership contingent upon a large personal contribution. Policies that make large gifts a requirement for board members are typically found in major performing arts organizations, large museums, and major hospitals. Other boards have a personal giving policy that presents options. The policy may state, for example, that each board member is expected either to personally contribute $10,000 or to raise that same amount from other people.

From time to time, a nonprofit organization may embark upon a capital campaign to purchase, expand, or renovate facilities. On such occasions, board members should be expected to make a major multiyear pledge that will yield sizable lead gifts that help get the campaign off the ground. The board's personal giving policy should note that capital campaign contributions are over and above those made annually.

For most boards, achieving 100 percent participation among board members is the goal. Hitting that mark enables an organization to justifiably boast that its own governing board is 100 percent behind the organization's work—and that's a big advantage when recruiting other donors. With the board as the role model for giving, others are more likely to follow suit.

To reach the 100 percent giving goal, some boards ask each member to sign a letter of intent for a specific gift amount. One board member then follows up with reminders to anyone who has not yet fulfilled his or her obligation. Others take a more informal approach simply by tracking the rate of participation among board members. The board chair may issue friendly reminders during meetings, therefore exerting peer pressure on those who have not yet contributed without mentioning anyone by name. The entire board should celebrate when it reaches the goal of 100 percent participation.

SUGGESTED ACTION STEPS

1. Board members, clearly articulate a board policy on personal giving; communicate it to new board members during recruitment and orientation and offer regular reminders to continuing board members.

2. Board members, designate a nonstaff person—perhaps the board chair or chair of the development committee—to follow up personally with those board members who have not yet made a gift.

PART
5

56.

How can we generate revenue beyond fundraising?

Does your organization's budget depend heavily on a signature activity or one big event, which could be easily affected by weather, timing, or competing activities? Is the biggest percentage of revenues tied to individual or corporate donations that vary from one year to the next? Diversifying the organization's income beyond direct fundraising can provide short-term economic stability as well as long-term viability (see Question 47).

Nonprofits have a variety of options for generating revenue, including the following.

Corporate sponsorships. For years, corporations have signed up to support a particular cause or effort. Eat a particular cereal, and you support the U.S. Olympic Team. Drink a specific brand of coffee, and you help save the rainforest. Purchase a certain piece of clothing, and you can aid a children's welfare organization. In fact, several research studies have confirmed that consumers are more likely to purchase products from companies that exhibit active community involvement. In addition, employees whose companies team up with nonprofits usually feel a greater loyalty to their employers.

Corporate sponsorships typically involve a specific product or signature event, although sometimes they apply to an organization's activities in general. They don't necessarily have to take the form of a cash donation. An airline, for example, may wish to provide corporate sponsorship by providing several round-trip tickets each year, which your organization can use as prizes. Some organizations have formalized corporate sponsorship programs with specified levels of involvement. That is, as a company invests more with the organization, it moves up the sponsorship ladder and in return receives additional recognition and public acknowledgments.

Note: The Internal Revenue Service keeps close watch on sponsorships, which, unlike advertising, are not subject to unrelated business income tax. Therefore recognition of sponsorships is allowed, provided it does not constitute advertising by granting substantial benefits to the company in return.

Affinity programs. Whether offered by credit card, car rental, or overnight shipping companies, affinity programs pay royalties to the nonprofits in return for use of their names, logos, and mailing lists. If someone carries a credit card with your organization's logo, for instance, you'll receive a royalty every time the card is used. These programs differ from sponsorships because they are not custom-crafted. Affinity programs typically offer a one-size-fits-all solution for which the nonprofit simply signs up as a participant.

Revenue-sharing programs. Found often on the Internet, these programs involve a merchant or retailer of goods and services paying a royalty or commission to the Web site's owner based on leads, referrals, or actual sales.

Licensing agreements. Through licensing, you give a company or another nonprofit the right to use the organization's intellectual property (such as a trademarked or copyrighted name, logo, slogan, or products) in exchange for royalties. Licensing agreements are often part of revenue-sharing and affinity programs, but they can stand on their own as well.

Cause-related marketing. In this situation, a corporation makes a designated contribution to the nonprofit organization every time a customer makes a particular purchase. A restaurant, for example, might donate $1 to your organization for every steak dinner it sells— or donate 1 percent of its total sales on a particular evening. Typically, the nonprofit organization is mentioned in the company's advertising and promotional materials, which can boost visibility of its mission.

Just be sure that you are not linking your organization's good name and reputation with a company that might undermine that very mission. For instance, a health-related organization probably wouldn't want to partner with a company connected to the manufacturing or distribution of tobacco or alcohol products. The connections are not always obvious, especially with multinational corporations, so research potential partners carefully before undertaking any cause-related marketing.

Entrepreneurial ventures. Your organization may have the expertise to launch its own business or commercial enterprise that addresses unmet needs within the community or sector. Often, a nonprofit's venture into the business marketplace is a natural extension of something it was already doing—such as a homeless shelter opening an employment agency. In fact, the board should ensure that any commercial or business venture supports or advances the main reason the organization exists.

Some organizations self-finance such a venture by drawing on their reserves or redirecting funds from another activity. Others take a pure business approach and obtain traditional bank financing, usually using reserves or building equity as collateral. You might even be able to tap into a venture philanthropy source—a funder that provides technical assistance or consulting, as well as dollars, to assist nonprofits with ventures that have a promise of sustainability for the long term. Such funding typically comes with specific conditions the nonprofit must meet.

PART
5

The board should ask staff to undertake a feasibility study, which includes preparing a financial analysis with projected expenses, revenues, implications for unrelated business income tax, and a break-even point for the business venture. These projections, when considered as part of your organization's financial picture, and the nature of the venture itself (how closely related it is to your mission and purpose) will help you decide whether setting up a for-profit subsidiary may be the best route to take (see Question 57). The feasibility study can form the foundation for a detailed business plan to guide the new venture.

Although the board must approve the policies governing the types of income-generating activities undertaken by the organization, it should hold the chief executive accountable for overseeing all those efforts. The chief executive's duties should include approving contracts, approving the promotional language and images used in marketing efforts, tracking royalty or sponsorship payments to the organization, and ensuring that corporate sponsors or supporters are properly acknowledged.

SUGGESTED ACTION STEPS

1. Board members, appoint a business ventures task group, consisting of staff, board members, and other stakeholders, to analyze the feasibility of generating revenues through other means.

2. Board members, benchmark what other nonprofits are doing in your community and across the nation. Discuss what lessons you have drawn from reviewing others' missteps and successes.

3. Board members, develop policies to guide staff members on such issues as selecting appropriate partners, using the organization's name and logo, and providing recognition.

4. Board members, before pursuing a business venture, require the staff to develop a full-blown business plan for presentation to board members and potential funders.

PART
5

57.

How do we, as a nonprofit, operate a for-profit subsidiary?

PART 5

Nonprofit organizations typically face this question when one of their activities unrelated to their tax-exempt purpose begins generating significant revenues. Such an unrelated, commercial activity can threaten the organization's tax-exempt status when it becomes substantial in comparison to exempt (related) activities.

Although the Internal Revenue Service (IRS) does not define "substantial," a general rule of thumb is to consult with your legal counsel and accounting firm when unrelated business activities generate more than one-third of your organization's income.

Unrelated Business Income Tax

Unrelated business activities that generate gross income of $1,000 or more annually may become subject to unrelated business income tax (UBIT). The Internal Revenue Service requires nonprofit organizations to pay UBIT on net income derived from activity that is

- A trade or a business, intended to generate income by selling goods or performing a service

- Regularly carried on, in a manner that mirrors the frequency and continuity of a similar activity conducted by a for-profit venture

- Unrelated to the performance of the nonprofit organization's tax-exempt purpose

For example, nonprofit organizations typically pay UBIT on income from sales of advertising in their publications and on income from the sale of merchandise that is not substantially related to the organization's purpose. (Sales of educational books may not be subject to UBIT, while sales of T-shirts or coffee mugs might be.) Investment income—revenue generated by royalties, dividends, and interest—is not subject to UBIT.

If your organization is subject to UBIT, ensure that detailed business records are kept; the costs directly associated with the unrelated business activity can be deducted. If unrelated business activities account for gross income of $1,000 or more, even if those activities produce a net loss after costs are deducted, your organization will need to file Form 990-T with the IRS. (After 2006, this tax return is a public document.)

PART
5

Good Reasons to Proceed

In addition to maintaining their tax-exempt status or reducing the amount of UBIT incurred, nonprofit organizations may want to create a for-profit subsidiary to do the following:

- *Limit their legal liability.* With appropriate controls in place, the parent organization can be shielded from the legal risks associated with the business activity. Because legal and regulatory requirements vary by state, be sure to consult your organization's legal counsel if this is a consideration.

- *Engage in a greater variety of activities.* The nonprofit's organizational documents or operating policies may restrict its ability to participate in the revenue-producing activities. These could then be undertaken by a standalone entity (either for-profit or nonprofit).

- *Better focus attention and resources.* By establishing a separate business, your organization is making a statement that it believes the activity is important. Whether the for-profit business involves publishing, insurance or employee benefits, financial services, group purchasing, or sales and marketing services, it will have its own staff, board of directors, and financial reporting requirements. This frees the parent organization to concentrate on other areas demanding attention.

- *Compete on a level playing field.* For-profit subsidiaries are better positioned to take on commercial competitors, which do not operate under strictures that may be imposed by a nonprofit organization. For instance, a magazine published by a subsidiary may be able to cover people or topics deemed too controversial by the parent organization; a subsidiary may be able to bring a product or service to the market much faster if it operates independently of the parent organization's formal budgeting and approval process.

PART
5

- *Reduce the likelihood of mixed messages.* A profitable business activity within the parent organization might raise eyebrows among those who believe a nonprofit organization should, at best, break even. Such an activity might also confuse potential members, community supporters, or donors who find that the reality of the organization's operations differs from their perceptions; they may believe the nonprofit enjoys an unfair advantage in the marketplace because of its tax-exempt status and thus should not compete with local businesses. Creating a for-profit subsidiary could help alleviate these impressions.

Setting Up Shop

For-profit subsidiaries tend to be established as corporations, with the parent organization owning at least 51 percent of its subsidiary's stock. Other people can also hold stock or equity in the spin-off corporation.

If, after consulting with legal counsel, your board believes a for-profit subsidiary will help generate revenue as well as provide valuable products or services, you'll need to take the steps necessary to spin off an activity. Bona fide intent should guide your decisions; in other words, you must make every effort to establish the subsidiary as an entity separate from the parent organization. Make sure to address the following areas.

Have a written agreement. A parent organization may have every intention of giving its for-profit subsidiary full independence. But directors and circumstances change, so formalizing the type of relationship between the two organizations can provide continuity and help resolve any issues that arise.

In the agreement, spell out the operational arrangement (facilities supplied, rent paid, and so forth), in addition to accountability and communication procedures. If, for instance, the parent organization grants full editorial freedom to its publishing subsidiary, the parent should not become involved if a stakeholder becomes upset about something that appeared in a newsletter or magazine; the publishing subsidiary should handle the matter.

Like any partnership, the relationship between a parent organization and its subsidiary depends on a high level of trust. Otherwise, each is likely to second-guess the other and create more problems than the subsidiary's establishment was intended to resolve. Maintaining this trust falls primarily to the chief executive officer of the parent organization.

Maintain independent boards, staff, and records. The nonprofit may appoint the subsidiary's board of directors, but by bringing in

PART
5

outsiders, the parent organization fosters independence between itself and the subsidiary.

Further, the subsidiary needs its own management team—some of whom may work for the parent organization as well. Staff members who work for both entities need to keep accurate records of their time and expenses. It's not unusual for a parent and its offspring organization to share employees and facilities, especially at the outset, but all those involved should record allocations of direct and overhead costs on a quarterly basis.

To be competitive in the marketplace, the subsidiary may have to offer higher salaries and incentive pay to attract staff members with for-profit experience. Be aware that this can be a bone of contention, and a morale issue, for the nonprofit's staff.

The subsidiary should also convene its own board meetings, keep minutes of those meetings, and have its own bank accounts and financial reports.

Exercise hands-off management. Even if a parent organization owns 100 percent of its subsidiary's stock or equity, it needs to take a hands-off approach to the subsidiary's day-to-day management and operations. A parent organization that exerts too much influence might lead the IRS to conclude that the subsidiary is not truly a separate entity, and that could lead to a loss of tax-exempt status.

Nonprofit Spin-Offs

Alternatively, a spin-off organization can, like its parent, be a nonprofit organization as well. For example, trade associations and professional societies sometimes create a separate 501(c)(3) entity to accept tax-deductible contributions for a specific educational or charitable purpose, such as awarding scholarships to students, providing community grants, or distributing educational materials.

Typically, a parent organization and its nonprofit subsidiary have interlocking, or overlapping, boards. The parent retains control over who serves on the subsidiary's board, often drawing on its own board or executive committee members to do double duty. Alternatively, the parent organization can take the ex officio approach, naming certain individuals (such as the chief executive and board chair) as ex officio members of the subsidiary board. Typically, the parent wants to control the majority of appointments to the board.

However similar their boards may be, the two organizations must maintain distinct operations. The parent organization's board may hold a meeting and then immediately reconvene as the subsidiary's board, but a separate agenda and separate minutes are required.

When boards overlap, it's advisable for the parent organization to further maintain control by requiring the subsidiary to request approval of any amendments to its governance documents (such as bylaws). The parent may also retain the right to remove any directors that it appointed to the subsidiary's board.

SUGGESTED ACTION STEPS

1. Board chair, ask an attorney and accountant to brief the board about the legal and financial advantages of establishing a for-profit or nonprofit subsidiary.

2. Board members, determine your organization's tolerance for financial risk: How soon would a new subsidiary be expected to show a return on investment?

3. Board members, appoint outsiders to serve on the board for any new subsidiary.

PART
5

QA

58.

What's the best way to keep track of board policies?

Given all the documents that you must review and act upon as a board member, it wouldn't be surprising if you had difficulty remembering which policies the board put into place during the previous meeting, let alone a year ago.

Providing a solution to policy confusion is simple: develop a board policy manual.

This manual houses all the ongoing policies that the board has adopted, organized for easy accessibility. The manual should be a fixture at every board meeting, providing the most up-to-date versions of board policies and decisions. Following are some reasons for this:

- The board is liable for its own policies in a court of law, so you need to know what the most current policies are.
- Board members waste time when they have to reinvent similar policies over and over again.

- Staff members need guidance on what policies they are expected to implement.

Whenever an issue surfaces, the first question to ask is, "What do our standing policies say?" If there is nothing in the board policy manual to guide the organization, the next question is, "What policy should we adopt to cover this and similar situations in the future?"

Developing a Policy Manual

Except for routine motions listed in the organization's minutes, the board policy manual should contain all standing policies of the organization as they have been added to or modified over time. Following are steps to developing such a manual.

Get the board to agree on the need. Most boards will acknowledge readily the problem of lost policies. Ultimately they must vote on the newly created standing policies, so they need to give their permission to start the task.

Review the hierarchy of legal authority. Each board member needs to understand where standing policies fit within the structure of other documents that guide the organization. The legal hierarchy is as follows:

A. Federal and state laws, including Internal Revenue Service regulations and legally binding contracts

B. Articles of incorporation for the organization

C. Bylaws of the organization

D. Standing policies of the organization

E. Other one-time, short-term resolution policies found in the board minutes

F. Administrative decisions made by staff, personnel policies, and procedures

An action at any level within this hierarchy may not violate the rules set in the level above it. If, for example, a board changes the organization's name as stated in the articles of incorporation, it must submit the change to the appropriate state authorities. The board can—and should—change its bylaws whenever they can be improved. Most boards do so every few years.

The board can add to, amend, or eliminate a specific standing policy whenever it finds a better way to state that policy.

Organize the manual into sections. A typical arrangement might be mission, board structure and process, finances, program, fundraising, board-staff relations, and the ever-necessary "miscellaneous." If you think through your own best table of contents, the writing task will be easier. But you can always rearrange the section headings once the project is under way.

Each chapter of the policies manual is based on the explicit understanding that someone has authority to make decisions within the context of the policies. Usually this person is the chief executive. In chapters relating to how the board functions, however, the board chair has the authority.

Assign people to draft policies for board review. Usually the chief executive is in the best position to do this because he or she thinks about the organization every day and is most aware of what's needed. Because setting board policy is the board's responsibility, however, a board-staff team of two also can be effective.

The drafters' initial task is to reflect, accurately and succinctly, the current policies of the organization. They should develop straightforward statements communicating current policy, whether found in the oral tradition or in the organization's documents (such as minutes, publications, or personnel manuals). Then they can identify any gaps to be addressed with new policies.

Write a first draft. If your organization has minutes containing clear, distinct policy resolutions, it may be possible to copy them directly into the policy manual's appropriate sections. This approach may not be possible if older policies pertain to specific issues and therefore offer little guidance for making decisions on other issues. The easiest approach then is to assemble the old policy statements as reference material (although they continue to be legally binding until superseded). They guide the drafting team in restating similar policies for the draft policies manual.

Policies should be clear, succinct, and free of legalese. They should not become so detailed that the board moves beyond policymaking and begins to invade staff administrative prerogatives.

Ask legal counsel to review the drafts. Once the drafting begins, bring the organization's legal counsel into the picture to review the document. The attorney should not write policies, but he or she certainly can suggest how best to adopt new policies and discontinue old, related policies.

Present drafts to the board for approval. Once the drafting team has sections ready for board approval, board members should provide informal feedback on the first reading. After incorporating the board's suggestions, the team should send the revised draft to members well in advance of the next board meeting.

PART
5

The board can formally adopt the standing policies manual as a whole document or one chapter or section at a time. Eventually, by resolution drafted by your legal counsel, terminate all previous policies that may conflict with these new ones.

Continue to review and revise board policies. After the major work is done, do not forget about standing policies. Use the policies manual as a resource. Continue to review policies for effectiveness. At some point, few policy changes will be required.

Creating a manual of board policies not only reduces confusion for board and staff but also promotes efficient governance and management. Staff members are free to initiate actions within the context of policies instead of taking every decision to the board for approval.

SUGGESTED ACTION STEPS

1. Board chair, ask your board what its policy is in two or three areas and when it was enacted. Illustrate the problem of forgotten policies by drawing from old minutes.

2. Board chair, bring to a board meeting a one-page draft relating to one aspect of the organization. Ask whether it reflects current practice. Does the board see the value of putting in writing what may only be assumed by some?

PART
5

PART SIX

Board-Staff Relations

Board members and staff members have the same goal: to help the organization achieve success by fulfilling its mission. They simply come at that goal from different perspectives and with different responsibilities. The board—led by the board chair—thinks and acts strategically, by setting the direction for the organization and establishing guidelines for it to follow. The staff—led by the chief executive—thinks and acts operationally, by finding the most efficient and effective means of implementing the board's direction within the guidelines.

The most successful organizations foster a "we're in this together" environment among board and staff. Both board members and staff members understand—and respect—their respective roles and responsibilities. When the lines between those responsibilities blur, as they sometimes do, the two groups work through any confusion amicably and productively.

$\mathcal{Q}_\mathcal{A}$ **59.**

Why should a nonprofit organization designate a chief executive?

Every nonprofit organization should designate one person to function as its operational leader. That person's title does not have to include the words *chief executive* or *chief executive officer*, but the bylaws and other policy documents should identify which position carries the authority and responsibility to run the organization day to day and reports to the board of directors. Following are some reasons why:

- *A board needs one point of accountability.* In nonprofit organizations, policy is always set by group action. No board member has more authority than other board members when it comes to establishing organizational directives. When policy is set, everyone must understand and agree upon who is responsible for implementing it.

    The chief executive also serves as the bridge between board and staff, whether paid or volunteer. He or she works closely with the board chair in setting board agendas and coordinating the staff work that supports the board in its governance job.

- *Staff members need to know where the buck stops.* Competition among staff members to determine who is in charge is distracting, if not destructive. Without a clear leader, a subtle competition for authority takes place among several people on the board and staff, and organizational matters suffer.

- *Donors need to identify the leader.* Donors enjoy giving to successful organizations. Many like to interact personally with the chief executive. People who give need confidence that the organization is in good hands—usually, one set of hands.

- *Other external constituencies need to know who's in charge.* When authority constantly shifts between the chair and the chief executive, no one knows who is in the position to make operational decisions. Some aspects of organizational life simply need the attention of the one person responsible for the whole. Banks, insurance companies, and vendors, for example, need the signature of the chief executive.

- *Planning needs a facilitator.* The chief executive is the natural person to coordinate an organization's planning process. Even when the board takes an active role and senior staff members do much of the work, planning breaks down without a chief executive to lead and to provide the continuity from planning to action.

- *The organization needs one spokesperson.* Although larger organizations may have a staff member with daily responsibility for public relations, the policy and the tone of what is distributed to the media and the public need clarity and continuity. That's why the chief executive often fills the role of chief spokesperson; in the event of a well-publicized change or crisis, the chief executive may move into the position of crisis coordinator (see Question 77).

Naming someone to function as the chief executive has everything to do with effectiveness, efficiency, productivity, high morale, and order. It is not a power play or a question of who is in a position to boss whom.

Potential Confusion

Terminology may create some confusion. Some nonprofits refer to their board chair as "president"; others reserve that title for their chief staff person. Unless the president's role is clarified and stated otherwise, the title may leave outsiders in a quandary as to whom they are dealing with. In general it makes sense to call the chair a chair, as that is clearly a board position.

Special challenges may be created by a founder who not only has written the formation documents but has left no doubt that he or she intends to run the organization. As there is no specific position called a "founder," this person has a tough choice to make: he or she will either chair the board as one of the board members or run the daily operations under the board's tutelage.

In the early stages, without a paid staff, the board has to handle both operational and governance duties. This situation calls for board members to be extra vigilant about which hat they wear under what circumstances (see Question 2). When they are involved in operations—such as planning and organizing a fundraising event—they must make decisions that are in line with board guidelines. When serving as board members, they must adjust their focus away from operational details and think and act strategically.

As nonprofit organizations grow and prosper, they hire a paid staff. Later, the nature or complexity of the organization or the qualities of the chief executive may call for designating the chief executive to oversee strategic priorities and provide overall leadership and a number-two executive (chief operating officer) to oversee administrative matters. This model works well, provided everyone is clear about who has executive authority for what. Exhibit 59.1 shows the difference in responsibilities between a chief executive officer and a chief operating officer.

PART
6

EXHIBIT 59.1. Chief Executive Officer Versus Chief Operating Officer.

CEO	COO
Is the leader	Is the manager
Does the right things	Does things right
Focuses on the long view	Focuses on the short view
Focuses on what and why	Focuses on how
Has vision and inspires others with it	Has hands-on control
Thinks future	Thinks present
Handles innovation and development	Handles administration
Sets tone and direction	Sets the pace
Relates to the COO and outside constituents	Relates to the CEO and inside constituents
Is accountable to a board	Is accountable to the CEO

SUGGESTED ACTION STEPS

1. Board members, check the organization's bylaws to see whether the designation of a chief executive is explicit and up to date.

2. Board members, if you have always considered the volunteer board chair, not the senior staff officer, to be the chief executive, consider whether the time is right to change that system.

Q&A

60.

What is the board's involvement in staff selection and management?

Boards become involved only in human resource matters that relate to the chief executive. The chief executive has the responsibility for handling human resource matters for all other staff members. That said, the board indirectly influences staff selection and management through the decisions it makes in guiding the organization. The board does this in the following ways.

Adopting policies. Human resource policies should address these questions, at a minimum:

- Does the board want to establish an organizational compensation level that is less than, equal to, or more than the average for similar organizations?
- To be competitive and reduce employees' taxes, to what extent does the organization want to be known for offering good

benefits? Specifically, how much of the cost should the organization bear for health, dental, vision, and life insurance? Should there be a pension plan, and what should the employee contribution be? Should the staff receive coupons for using public transportation? Should there be free parking?

- Should there be an emphasis on promoting from within?

- Does the board endorse performance-based compensation?

- Should human resource policies encourage long-term employment, or should the board assume a three- to four-year tenure?

- To what extent should the organization plan its services to tap as much volunteer staff as possible? Should the organization reimburse volunteers' expenses?

Modeling the policies with the chief executive. How the board recruits, compensates, evaluates, and terminates the chief executive speaks volumes to staff members who are involved in human resource matters with other staff members. Obviously, the board should follow its own policies in how it deals with the chief executive (see Questions 64 and 65).

Delegating all other human resource decisions to the chief executive. If it were to become involved in hiring and compensation decisions for senior staff members, a board would risk undermining the chief executive's authority and marginalizing its expectations of staff loyalty and trust. Besides, the board is far too removed from day-to-day operations to be able to make choices, set salary levels, and evaluate staff members they see just a few times a year. Successful delegation of this authority to the chief executive, however, requires that the board clearly articulate its philosophy of staffing and fulfill its legal obligations. For instance, the board should review the compensation packages for all senior staff members whose compensation is reported on Form 990 (see Question 54).

Deciding budget issues relating to the staff. The board can decide what percentage increase the new budget should include for staff salaries, but the chief executive is in the best position to determine how to allocate that amount among across-the-board increases, merit increases, or adjustments to keep up with the market. Within the budget, the board could also specify limits on items such as health insurance or contributions to retirement accounts.

Monitoring staffing. The board should ask for reports on matters such as staffing levels, salaries, evaluation procedures, and management of incentive pay. If the board sees things that are potentially damaging to the organization, it should revise its policies and expect the chief executive to make corresponding changes. Of course, a good chief executive checks informally with board members before making any major decisions that are likely to trouble the staff.

A board can adjust its role in human resource matters depending on the organization's needs. For example, perhaps the chief executive wants the finance committee to interview the top three candidates for the chief financial officer position. The committee can provide useful feedback, but the decision belongs to the chief executive, to whom the chief financial officer would report.

The staff should feel good if the board is clear on general policies, treats the chief executive fairly, expects all human resource decisions to comply with the law, raises sufficient funds for equitable salaries, and then lets the chief executive manage the staff needed to accomplish the organization's mission. When boards delve more deeply into the specifics of how staff members are hired, trained, compensated, evaluated, or terminated, both the staff and the board ultimately suffer.

PART
6

SUGGESTED ACTION STEPS

1. Board members, review the policies governing human resource matters. Do some require clarification or revision?

2. Chief executive, if the board seems too involved in selecting staff or setting salaries, ask a neutral consultant to interview staff and board members to assess the impact of the board's role and make suggestions.

61.

Should the chief executive have a vote on the board?

Among the nonprofit organizations that responded to a Board-Source survey, 82 percent do not grant the chief executive a vote on the board. Still, most organizations welcome the chief executive as a member of the board by virtue of his or her office.

Some boards grant full voting rights to the chief executive—particularly one who was a founder, incorporated the organization, and helped recruit the first board members. Others acquiesce to the demands of a new chief executive who, by virtue of age and experience, insists upon having a vote as a condition of employment. These situations, however, point to governance problems and confusion over appropriate roles.

Even as a founder, a chief executive should remain focused on operational issues and helping to build a board that can fulfill its role independently. And an effective, confident chief executive feels secure in the role of staff leader rather than looked down upon by board peers just because he or she does not sit on the board. In addition, the chief executive's job is to support the board by implementing its decisions. He or she needs to maintain the confidence and trust of the entire board, building relationships that promote effective interaction. The chief executive should never be put in the position of having to vote against any board member.

Instead, chief executives who are given a seat on the board usually serve ex officio and without a vote. They can participate in discussions and provide information, but the final decision rests with the volunteer leaders wearing their governance hats.

Even without a vote, chief executives have influence over board decisions. Their perspective is instrumental. Every chief executive should sit next to the chair during all business meetings (except executive sessions) and have the right to speak as a board member. In fact, most questions during debate are directed to the chief executive. When handled wisely, this power can exceed most board members' abilities to influence board or organizational policies.

SUGGESTED ACTION STEPS

1. Board members, ensure that the organization's bylaws clearly state whether the chief executive is a nonvoting member of the board.

2. Board chair, involve the chief executive in meeting preparations and discussions and solicit his or her opinion before calling for a vote.

PART
6

Q_A

62.

Should board members be hired as staff members?

There is nothing wrong with an organization hiring someone who happens to sit on its board, provided two principles are observed:

- The organization follows an open process that results in hiring the most qualified candidate.
- The candidate resigns from the board.

In short, no board member should serve simultaneously on the staff except for the chief executive. A stronger board policy might even be called for—for example, no board member may accept a paid position with the organization unless he or she has been off the board for one year.

There are simply too many conflicts of interest for a board member, other than the chief executive, to serve on the board. Besides, a staff member who attends meetings as a board member and then returns to staff meetings is bound to create morale problems with other staff members.

What should your organization do if some board members already work as paid employees? Ideally, the board chair will ask the board members to step down from one of their positions. At a minimum, the board chair and chief executive should draft guidelines that could prevent embarrassing situations in the future. Examples include the following:

- Board members who are also employees may not discuss board business with staff members other than as required by the chief executive.
- These individuals must maintain confidentialities in both settings, as appropriate.
- These individuals must excuse themselves from any specific board discussion when they, the chair, the chief executive, or any two members of the board suggest that they leave.

Two other dimensions to this issue remain. First, many nonprofit organizations have volunteers who carry significant responsibilities. It should not be a problem for board members to volunteer for one of these tasks. Second, it may be acceptable to retain a board member as a paid consultant for a short-term assignment following an open selection process and enforcement of the conflict-of-interest policy.

SUGGESTED ACTION STEPS

1. Board chair, if a board member other than the chief executive serves on the paid staff, ask a neutral consultant to interview board and staff members confidentially about the situation and summarize their comments in a report to the board.

2. Board members, if your organization does not have a "no staff on the board" policy, develop a simple statement that puts the responsibility on the shoulders of each board member to resign if he or she is offered—or even wants to apply for—a staff position.

PART
6

QA

63.

How should we evaluate the chief executive?

All staff and board members should be able to answer five basic questions about their individual jobs:

1. What am I expected to do?
2. Why is it important?
3. Do I have authority to do it?
4. When I need help, where can I go?
5. How am I doing so far?

A chief executive may have difficulty answering that last question if the board, as a group, has never spelled out the goals against which his or her leadership could be evaluated. The chief executive is left trying to read board members' minds—and each board member may expect something different from his or her performance. When the chief executive isn't clear about what the board expects, the whole organization may lack focus, suffer low morale, and consequently be less effective.

A planned, thoughtful approach to evaluating the chief executive removes confusion. Determining evaluation criteria for the chief executive enables all members of the board to operate on the same assumptions and have the same expectations about the organization's direction and priorities. In addition, when the board and chief executive agree on their priorities, staff members usually receive clearer directions for their work and their own performance evaluations.

This evaluation of the chief executive should take place annually and be initiated by the board chair or other officer, and if that does not happen, the chief executive should take the initiative and remind the board of its responsibility. Often, the chief executive contributes to the process by drafting a summary or clarification of annual expectations to begin the performance discussion.

How to Evaluate

Performance evaluations can range from short conversations with board officers to a full-blown assessment that uses an outside consultant. What is right for your organization usually becomes evident once the board chair and the chief executive agree on a general approach. Here are some tips:

- Develop the evaluation process and schedule as a team (the board and the chief executive working together).

- Separate the evaluation process from salary negotiations, which should come later.

- Restrict the board to evaluating only the chief executive.

- Appoint a two- or three-person ad hoc committee of skilled board members to conduct the evaluation.

- With input from the entire board, create an evaluation form with both quantifiable and open-ended questions.

PART
6

- As the situation requires it, decide whether to interview staff members. (*Note:* This should rarely be necessary and should happen only with the chief executive's knowledge.)

- Invite the chief executive to write a self-evaluation as part of the process.

- Give the chief executive an opportunity to discuss items and ask for clarification on the evaluation committee's comments, both positive and negative.

- Have the evaluation committee report to the entire board, after debriefing the chief executive. For legal purposes, a written record of the evaluation must be kept on file.

- Write an "evaluation of the evaluation" for the files so the process can be consistent and even more effective the next time.

- Write performance criteria for the next year's evaluation, to be mutually agreed upon by the board and chief executive.

What to Evaluate

The evaluation should cover all aspects of the chief executive's performance in helping the organization accomplish the expectations the board has established. (This is not difficult to do if the board is clear about the organization's mission.) For instance, board evaluation committees commonly ask whether the chief executive's leadership has accomplished the following goals:

- Created positive relationships with board members and helped strengthen the board

- Built a strong internal organization in which systems, staff productivity and morale, and teamwork have improved

- Advanced the quality and increased the quantity of the services provided

- Increased the public's trust in the organization's integrity
- Improved financial resources and accountability

The evaluation process can improve communications, boost the level of trust among board members and the chief executive, and enhance the ability to work in harmony. Honesty and sincerity on the board's part inevitably lead to a better organization and a more productive relationship with the chief executive.

SUGGESTED ACTION STEPS

1. Board members, review what the bylaws or board policies say, what the chief executive was told when hired, and when the last formal evaluation was completed.
2. Board members, develop a formal process and timetable for annually evaluating the chief executive's performance; the process should include appointing an evaluation committee or task force with several board members.

PART
6

64.

How do we set fair compensation for the chief executive and the staff?

Few, if any, nonprofit professionals get paid as much as those doing similar work in the business community. Typically, nonprofit boards want to pay competitive wages so they can attract top talent but not exceed the salary guidelines of similar organizations.

Following are some questions to ask when setting guidelines for compensation decisions.

What is our financial strength? You can't pay more than you have. Payroll and program costs must be in a reasonable balance to fulfill your charitable purpose. You should have a reserve account of at least 10 to 12 percent of your operating budget so you can pay salaries when cash flow is down. If you are struggling financially, you may not be able to pay what the salary surveys say is average.

What is our philosophy about compensation? A board should reflect on what kind of nonprofit entity it governs and how donors and moral owners feel about compensation in your sector. Staff in social services organizations, for example, seldom make what their counterparts do in health-related organizations. Donors to religious organizations do not expect employees to earn what business trade associations might pay. Once the board realizes what is publicly acceptable, however, it still needs to determine philosophically whether it would like its employees to be near the mean or median, or in the upper quarter of similar organizations.

What can we learn from salary surveys? You can obtain state, regional, and national surveys conducted by either nonprofit associations or private firms. The data from such surveys typically offer overall averages as well as salaries reported according to budget size, staff size, and type or scope of organization. Although useful, salary surveys should not be the sole means of setting compensation because sample size and other variables can influence the results.

What is our goal? Some boards decide salaries are less than what they would like them to be. They set a goal—say, to have salaries reflect approximately 80 percent of salaries in similar jobs in the local business market. It may take three years or more to reach this goal, but board members and staff could be motivated to find the financial means to meet it. In addition, a board should have this kind of framework within which to plan.

Who determines specific salaries? The board should set only the chief executive's compensation but carefully review the senior staff members' compensation. Then the chief executive, within budget guidelines, should determine the rest of the payroll. The chief executive is in the best position to know what it takes to recruit and keep good people. Staff members should feel that someone who knows their work is setting their compensation.

Should we use performance-based compensation? Taking a cue from the corporate world, more nonprofits are offering merit-based

PART
6

pay that links salaries, bonuses, or both to job performance. Acknowledging that this practice can complicate compensation calculations and create internal competition, the chief executive should set some guidelines. For example, will bonuses be considered for work groups in addition to, or instead of, individual performance ratings? Should cost-of-living adjustments be dropped entirely? Should performance pay increase the base salary or be paid in one-time, lump-sum bonuses? Approximately what percentage of the staff should receive performance raises? By how much should the highest merit increase exceed the smallest merit increase? These are all value judgments a chief executive should explore in detail, with broad guidance from the board. However, percentage-based compensation should never be considered in a nonprofit.

Merit-based compensation can work well as a small part of the total compensation program if the staff has a role in deciding the pros and cons. If staff members help create a system for rewarding performance, they may be more open to the idea that those who go the extra mile should be rewarded, or that measuring performance is a good strategy for accomplishing the organization's mission. They may agree that people should be allowed to compete for something extra in a nonprofit organization that pays modest salaries. This discussion takes place at the staff level, facilitated by the chief executive and possibly an outside expert.

For its part, the board must support merit-based efforts, monitor the results, and understand the criteria for awarding bonuses. The board should apply the same criteria when deciding how to compensate the chief executive.

What kind of compensation can we offer besides cash? From the board's perspective, the total outlay for employees should be more important than how benefits are distributed. For the chief executive in particular, it may be preferable to provide a lower salary and greater benefits, such as additional health and life insurance, deferred compensation, coverage of educational expenses, an annual executive physical exam, a sabbatical, or use of a vehicle.

PART 6

Chief Executive Compensation

Remember, the organization's mission demands effective leadership, not just average management—and that requires a financial investment. Even in a nonprofit it is totally appropriate to compensate a qualified leader in a fair manner that acknowledges positive results and feeds into job retention. However, the board needs to pay attention to overcompensation. The Internal Revenue Service can assess intermediate sanctions on board members and managers who approve or receive "excess benefits," or unreasonable compensation for their work or service (see Question 7).

Consult with legal counsel to ensure that your organization is taking the appropriate action to avoid excess-benefit transactions in the area of executive compensation (including health benefits, retirement benefits, incentive plans, and other perquisites).

SUGGESTED ACTION STEPS

1. Board chair, ask the chief executive to gather and summarize for the board facts and trends about staff compensation in your field.

2. Board members, identify the five nonprofit organizations most comparable to your own. Check their most recent Form 990s at www.guidestar.org so you can compare compensation levels.

3. Board chair, purchase a national compensation survey for board education purposes.

4. Board chair, engage an outside expert to review your current policies and practices and make recommendations to the board.

PART
6

Q_A

65.

What is the chief executive's role in improving the board?

A proper balance must be struck between the board doing its work independently and the other extreme, in which the chief executive forges ahead with little or no regard for the board's wishes or expectations. As in all human interaction, trust is key. The board needs to perceive that the chief executive is sincerely helping it to be all that a good board should be.

For certain, no board can be effective when it feels it is competing with the chief executive and not getting the support it needs. So the chief executive needs to make developing the board a priority. This includes meeting with prospective board members, orienting new members, meeting individually with the chair and other board members, preparing for meetings, and doing the follow-up every board meeting requires. In fact, some chief executives say they devote as much as 20 percent of their time to board relations.

The key point is that all boards require leadership from their chief executive to do their work well. Therefore, as a board member, you should expect the chief executive to do the following:

- *Be a student of nonprofit governance.* No other staff or board member is likely to be as motivated to learn common principles and emerging trends related to boards. Many good print resources and workshops on board issues are available.

- *Train the board.* Most members bring differing opinions about what the board should or should not do. For consistency, each organization needs to develop written policies regarding how it handles its governing tasks. The chief executive has an instrumental role in helping the board reach consensus positions on a range of structural and role issues.

- *Help shape standing policies.* Based on the agenda prepared with the board chair, the chief executive must anticipate which critical issues will require board action and draft motions accordingly. When a motion is carefully articulated and distributed in writing, the board can deal with it much more thoughtfully. Even with a few amendments, it will become part of the policy manual.

- *Help recruit new board members.* Finding the people with the right qualifications at the right time for the organization takes a lot of effort. The chief executive has the most at stake in finding qualified people who know enough about the organization to make a wise decision about serving as a board member. Effective chief executives keep a list of prospective board members and pull those people into the organization's volunteer activities.

- *Insist on board-friendly staff reports.* What works best for the staff often does not work best for boards. Chief executives can facilitate the governance process by helping staff members develop reports and issue papers that suit the needs of volunteer

PART
6

board members. Materials should be in context and as brief as possible. They should explain pros and cons, present a clear recommendation if called for, and respond to board concerns expressed in the past.

A chief executive can help focus the board on governance by working with the board chair to do the following:

- *Periodically review progress on the strategic plan.* Emphasize how the chief executive, in conjunction with staff, carries out the board's decisions. The report should focus on where the organization is headed, as determined by the board, and how that goal will be achieved, as determined by the chief executive.

- *Structure meeting agendas to minimize operational reports.* Offer to supply comprehensive supporting documents later should board members request more details. Group housekeeping items, such as approval of previous minutes and committee appointments, in a consent agenda. This frees up time for higher-level discussion. In fact, some chief executives include two or three strategic questions under each agenda item to get board members thinking in advance about what comments or feedback to offer.

- *Aim for a give-and-take dialogue between staff members and the board at meetings.* Instead of having staff members answer a string of detailed questions fired off by board members, the chief executive can facilitate discussion and summarize the strategic points made by board members, perhaps by politely asking, "Where are we right now in the discussion? How do these comments relate to the strategic issue at hand?"

- *Develop visual indicators of organizational performance.* Consider using the dashboard concept to help the board easily gauge progress or identify potential problem areas. Just like the dashboard on a car, a nonprofit dashboard provides a quick glimpse of important information, such as progress on a capital campaign, the number of new donors, and client satisfaction ratings. The information appears in a short, easy-to-view format, defined by charts, graphs, or comparison data from previous years. Some organizations even code each item on the dashboard as having a green light (goal reached or in sight), a yellow light (area to watch with caution), or a red light (requires action now).

- *Integrate a board development activity into every meeting.* This may range from a presentation by an outside financial expert or staff program specialist to an overview of funding within your community to a personal story shared by a client or member served by the organization. Another option is to break the board into smaller groups for roundtable discussions on topics related to mission and vision, then reconvene to process the information that emerged from the brainstorming.

- *Evaluate the board's own performance.* Some groups do a quick check-in after every meeting or two, asking board members to rate, on a continuum, the level of discussion (operational versus strategic), the issues covered (trivial versus significant), and the materials provided (useless versus useful). Others periodically ask community members, staff, and clients or customers to provide feedback on how well the organization appears to be governed.

SUGGESTED ACTION STEPS

PART
6

1. Chief executive, encourage each board member to read a book or other resource materials related to nonprofit governance.

2. Board members, participate with the chief executive in a brainstorming session on how each could help improve the board.

Q A

66.

What is the board's role in relation to the staff?

A loose organizational style, in which board members pitch in to get the work done in the office and staff members institute policies without board approval, blurs the line between the board's and staff's unique roles within the organization. It can also lead to legal liability, if boards are not making and carefully documenting policy decisions.

But the most compelling reason to distinguish between board and staff responsibilities relates to organizational effectiveness. Everyone becomes more productive when board and staff members do not spend time doing one another's work. The best boards stick to wearing their "governance hats" when assembled for a business meeting with a quorum present (see Question 2). When doing board work, some formality is both legally and practically appropriate.

Exhibit 66.1 illustrates key differences between the board and the chief executive.

The first order of business in sorting out roles is to put everything in writing. Oral tradition does not work well in nonprofit governance. People bring different experiences to the boardroom and translate

EXHIBIT 66.1. Distinct Roles of the Board and the Chief Executive.

The Board	The Chief Executive
Is corporate; acts as a group	Is individual
Is continuous	Is temporary
Is part-time	Is full-time
Has no staff or minimal staff	Has access to all staff
Has ultimate responsibility	Has limited, immediate responsibility
Is typically not expert in the work of the organization	Is typically professional and an expert in this arena
Gives volunteer time	Earns a salary
See only parts of the whole	Is intimately involved in everything

them into different assumptions about what should happen. Then turnover of board members and staff adds to the confusion. The result: miscommunication, misunderstandings, and mistakes.

Together, the board and the chief executive should clarify their respective roles within the organization and record them in simple, straightforward terms. That enables people involved in the organization now, and in the future, to refer to a consistent set of expectations. Completing the worksheet in Exhibit 66.2 can help you arrive at those expectations and determine how far the organization still needs to travel.

SUGGESTED ACTION STEPS

1. Board members, during an open discussion, identify any areas of confusion between board and staff roles. Clarify who does what, and formalize those decisions in policy statements.

2. Board members, invite an objective consultant to observe several board and staff meetings. Ask for feedback on areas needing clarification of roles and responsibilities.

PART
6

EXHIBIT 66.2. Board and Staff Roles Worksheet.

For each issue or task, indicate with the appropriate letter where your board is now and where it should be:

A. Board initiates and decides on its own (chief executive may implement).

B. Chief executive formally recommends and board decides.

C. Chief executive decides or acts after consultation with board members during or outside of normal board or committee meetings.

D. Chief executive, staff members, or both act on their own within approved guidelines.

Issues and Tasks	Is Now	Should Be
1. Mission statement for organization		
2. Formal annual goals and objectives		
3. Recruitment of new board members		
4. Board and committee structure		
5. Policies regarding board role and activities		
6. Hiring and salaries of staff other than chief executive		
7. Changes in bylaws to keep current		
8. Annual income and expense budget		
9. Budget amendments as required		
10. Capital expenditures		
11. Staff compensation policies		
12. Other personnel policies and practices		
13. Investment policies		
14. Arrangements for external audit		
15. Fundraising plan and policies		
16. Adoption of new programs or services		
17. Termination of current programs or services		
18. Staff organizational structure		
19. Organization's insurance program		
20. Board meeting agendas		
21. Other:		

Q A **67.**

How can the senior staff contribute to board effectiveness?

The chief executive has the sole responsibility for implementing the board's directives. Still, senior staff members play key roles in helping both the chief executive and the board do their work well. Following are ways in which they can help:

- *Provide informative reports to the chief executive.* Good written reports from the senior staff, sent to the full board a couple of weeks in advance of their meetings, educate board members and prepare them for dialogue. Then there is no need to take up precious board meeting time with oral reports. Reports should be brief (no more than two pages), put issues in context, and indicate how board policies are working. The chief executive can summarize staff reports in his or her report to the board.

- *Attend board meetings.* In addition to assisting board members with presentations, staff members are available to answer on-the-spot questions from board members (when requested to do so by the chief executive). They hear firsthand the concerns of the board and see how their leader explains the issues. Finally, being in the boardroom reduces some of the mystery and anxiety surrounding the governance process. Staff members see that board members are ordinary people doing their best to help fulfill the organization's mission.

After the board meeting, the chief executive benefits from hearing the perspectives of each staff member. When the board has made significant policy changes, the key people know the importance of adjusting to the new direction because they were present for the board discussion. They are better able to explain board actions to their own staffs.

- *Create tracking systems.* The board often asks the staff to help establish the means of evaluating how well the organization is reaching key goals. Good data are essential to good governance, and boards depend on staff members to gather and present the data in an understandable manner.

- *Support the work of committees.* Many boards have committees that relate closely to one or more senior staff assignments. Staff members naturally become the primary resource for committee chairs as they plan agendas or prepare special reports. Some may serve as staff liaisons to the appropriate committees. In this role, the staff can help committees focus on board issues, not staff responsibilities.

- *Respond to inquiries.* Although board members should not request information that is primarily of personal interest, staff members should be prepared to give information to board officers and committee chairs between meetings. The board should channel these requests through the chief executive so he or she is aware of the information needs.

- *Work as a team.* Board members observe how well staff members get along, work together, and are loyal to the mission and one another. Staff members who "end run" the chief executive, betray confidences to board members during informal conversations, or talk negatively about their colleagues are not exhibiting professional behavior or earning the board's trust.

- *Build relationships.* Social exchanges between individual senior staff and board members can build mutual respect as well as board effectiveness. Senior staff and board members can have meaningful friendships as long as those friendships are not used inappropriately when it comes to the work of the organization.

- *Lead by modeling.* Committees are meant to help the board— not the staff—do its work. Committee members in particular can fall into the trap of advising staff members while neglecting to formulate recommendations for board action. Staff members need to model the governance process by not encouraging board members or committees to compromise their job descriptions. They can get advice from anywhere, including some board members, but that activity needs to fall outside of governance work.

- *Identify prospective board members.* Although the board is responsible for defining and identifying good board prospects, it should solicit suggestions from the senior staff. Staff members often know volunteers and donors who have the proper qualifications to serve on the board.

Remember: the staff and the board are not in competition. When each group understands the potential for positive interaction and works to make the other stronger and more effective, everyone helps advance the organization's mission.

PART
6

SUGGESTED ACTION STEPS

1. Board chair, ask board members or executive committee members to give the chief executive their thoughts on how

the senior staff is, or is not, being used to advance the work of the board.

2. Board members, have the chief executive ask senior staff members to evaluate their own attitudes about and experience with board relations, coming to consensus on how to improve.

Q

68.

How can we facilitate the end of a chief executive's employment?

Perhaps the annual evaluation process uncovers some doubts about the chief executive's ability to effectively lead the organization (see Question 63). Maybe the chief executive is approaching the age of retirement or has found a new employment opportunity that offers greater professional fulfillment. Or maybe the chief executive's skills were better suited for a different phase in the organization's lifecycle that has since passed (see Question 71).

Whatever the reason and motivation, a chief executive's departure from the organization can be unsettling. As a result, the board must exercise care, forthrightness, grace, and sensitivity to the needs of the person and the organization. Although the executive or governance committee frequently conducts performance and compensation reviews on behalf of the board, all board members should be involved in any transitions of the one staff member who reports to them.

In this chapter are suggestions for dealing with specific situations that your organization may encounter. How the board manages the loss of a key player in each of these situations will affect the whole organization.

Retirement

When a long-standing chief executive reaches age sixty or so, he or she is probably wondering about the best time to retire. An alert board is probably thinking about the same thing. More often than not, the answer is a result of honest conversations between the chief executive and the board chair and perhaps other board members.

It is common for a board, perhaps during the chief executive's annual evaluation, to raise the issue of retirement. Many factors may feed into this: an upcoming capital campaign, a merger, a move to a different location, the planned retirement of another staff veteran. If the chief executive is interested in retirement but unsure of the timing, the board might offer a sabbatical prior to retirement.

Job Change

The chief executive may simply announce his or her departure to take another job, although the decision should be communicated first to the board chair. Together, the two leaders can work out the timing of the staff executive's departure and transition details.

If the chief executive has many loyal supporters within the organization and the community, the board may sponsor a reception in the person's honor and provide a thank-you gift. To recognize the contributions of especially effective chief executives, some organizations name awards or sponsor events in their honor.

Forced Resignation

A nonprofit board may conclude that some action or inaction on the part of the chief executive requires that person's fairly quick departure from the organization. The chair is asked to deliver a blunt message: "For these reasons, the board wants to give you the option of resigning at the end of this month or being fired on Friday." Most chief executives would prefer to resign and have some influence over how the announcement is made.

This is never easy and seldom a pleasant way to fulfill the board's responsibility to the organization's stakeholders. The local media or the organization's newsletter often will explain that there are "personal reasons" for the departure. Most people will know that this tactic simply puts a nice spin on being fired, but it is a good option that protects the organization from negative press and leaves some dignity to the chief executive and his or her family.

If the situation leading up to the termination has potential legal ramifications, often an attorney will be asked to draft a memorandum of understanding that spells out what the board or the chief executive can say in public about the situation.

An emotional whirlwind usually accompanies a chief executive's sudden departure. The staff, the board, and the departing chief executive all need time to overcome the tension, anger, frustration, doubt, guilt, and anxiety that come with the situation.

Termination

When a chief executive is fired, he or she often has made decisions or statements that have riled the public—or at least enough donors and supporters—to create a crisis. Staff members may be threatening to leave. A foundation may want to pull back on its funding. An aggrieved employee may have gone public with some indiscretion on the part of the chief executive. Whatever the reason, for the integrity and progress of the organization, the board realizes that everyone is looking to it to act (see Question 77). To exercise good trusteeship, the board must take on the least pleasant task of firing the chief executive.

If this situation arises in your nonprofit, the board must

- Unanimously support the decision to terminate employment of the chief executive; the decision would probably be made during an executive session or during a board conference call if the decision must be made without delay.

PART
6

- Make sure the action never comes as a surprise to the chief executive. Have substantial documentation of the performance or lack of performance that led to the action.

- Tell the chief executive first. Do not "leak" the news to anyone else.

- Ask an attorney to draft a mutually agreeable termination document. This will reduce the possibility of costly legal battles.

- Communicate the decision. The board chair should brief staff on who will be the acting chief executive and send a letter to donors and special friends. A press release may also be in order.

- Quickly initiate the process to find a replacement (see Question 70).

Succession Planning

Even if your organization's chief executive is young, healthy, and still passionate about the job, you need to have a back-up plan. Succession planning is especially critical for younger organizations so they don't crumble if suddenly confronted with the loss of the staff leader who keeps the day-to-day operations running smoothly. It entails five steps.

Be clear on the chief executive's role. All board members should understand their responsibilities and how those of the chief executive differ (see Questions 1 and 59). Knowing the multiple roles played by the chief executive will help the board focus on the type of person the job requires and the demands it asks of that person. The board should have ready access to an updated job description for the chief executive.

Agree on expectations. Rather than wait for the chief executive's evaluation to roll around each year, both the chief executive and board members—particularly the board chair—should frequently discuss and reach agreement on their respective roles and responsibilities.

Who needs what from whom—and by when? Achieving and maintaining this clarity leads to open conversations and a healthy partnership. It also reduces the likelihood that tension and disagreements between the parties will escalate into conflicts that become difficult, if not impossible, to resolve.

Conduct a board self-assessment. Turnover in staff leadership provides a natural point for the board to look at its own performance vis-à-vis the chief executive. But even at other times, introspection helps a board become more productive (see Question 36). In fact, boards that conduct periodic self-assessments typically have the knowledge and confidence to weather a staff leadership transition smoothly.

Establish an evaluation process for the chief executive. The question of a chief executive's future plans should be a routine part of his or her annual performance review (see Question 63). Asking, "Where do you see yourself in five years?" doesn't imply that the board has plans that don't include the chief executive. Rather, it confirms the board's interest in the chief executive's professional and personal development and reduces the likelihood that the board will be caught unprepared for a retirement or resignation.

PART
6

Create an emergency transition plan. Have a contingency plan in place to guide both board and staff in the event of the chief executive's departure or long-term absence. The plan, for example, might enable the board to appoint an interim chief executive from among the senior staff members. Some executives find it fulfilling to mentor younger colleagues who, subject to the board's wishes, may one day be able to step directly into the chief executive's position on a temporary or permanent basis.

If the board determines that no senior staff member has the appropriate qualifications or experience to lead the organization during the transition, it may have a policy to hire a consultant or other seasoned manager to serve as the interim executive director.

SUGGESTED ACTION STEPS

1. Board chair, after talking with the chief executive, board and staff members, and other stakeholders, invite an outside, objective evaluator to provide an analysis that helps answer the question of chief executive tenure.

2. Board members, when a chief executive nears retirement age, encourage a private conversation between the executive committee and the chief executive about the near-term future. This could be a routine question in the annual evaluation.

3. Board members, well in advance of a leadership void, develop policies addressing succession planning, severance benefits, search and transition guidelines, and related issues.

Q
A

69.

What characteristics should we look for in a new chief executive?

If you gathered ten chief executives in one room, you'd undoubtedly encounter dynamic visionaries as well as quiet managers, and no-nonsense commanders as well as easy-going delegators. Yet despite a diversity of personalities and individual skills, chief executives need to have a board-centered leadership style.

According to Robert D. Herman and Richard D. Heimovics, writing in *Executive Leadership in Nonprofit Organizations: New Strategies for Shaping Executive-Board Dynamics* (Jossey-Bass, 1991), a board-centered leadership style calls for

PART
6

- Facilitating interaction in board relationships
- Showing consideration and respect toward board members
- Envisioning change and innovation with the board
- Promoting board accomplishments and productivity

- Initiating and maintaining a structure for board work
- Providing helpful information to the board

No one person can meet all the expectations a group of people may have, so a board must say what it believes are the essentials for leading the organization. Organizations need a different style of executive leadership at different stages of growth, and more than one leadership style could work in your organization at any given time.

Consider the following characteristics and determine which ones are most essential to your organization at this point in its lifecycle (see Question 71).

Vision bearer.   The chief executive must be skilled at articulating and promoting the vision and mission that guide the organization. People follow men and women who know where they are going.

In startup organizations, the chief executive is often the founder and keeper of the vision that attracts board members, volunteers, and donors. The vision creates excitement. Sustaining that initial excitement depends heavily on the chief executive. In a mature organization—one that has had, say, five or more chief executives—the chief executive must sometimes move slowly in changing the vision because so many are now aware of it and believe in it. But he or she must embrace the vision and find new ways for people to relate to it.

Persuasive or motivational.   A chief executive, by definition, must motivate other people to accomplish activities in support of the vision or mission. A board needs a chief executive who can explain, persuade, and empower others to do their best. Paid and volunteer staff members need to know why they do what they do. Donors must understand the purpose and the opportunity to help financially.

Many different styles seem to work for chief executives in meeting this test. Some quietly model what they want others to see and follow. Many are particularly gifted at oral persuasion or at wielding a creative pen. A few can persuade by the sheer strength of their domineering personalities, although depending on guilt, intimidation, or obligation is typically a short-term leadership style.

Motivation comes after the first wave of enthusiasm. Being a good persuader and being a motivator go hand in hand.

Ethical. The best chief executives don't stop at what they perceive to be expected ethical behavior. They go the extra mile, challenging board members, staff, and donors to be above reproach in all areas.

Many ethical traps lurk for participants in a nonprofit organization. Sometimes a law is misunderstood; sometimes a donor tempts one to compromise in return for a gift. Friends may ask favors they shouldn't get. But people see the successful chief executive as committed to what is good and honest. When mistakes are uncovered, this type of chief executive is willing to face the music and correct what is wrong.

Focused on strengths. Top chief executives do not try to do all things or be all things. They focus on their strengths to achieve the productivity they enjoy and manage their weaknesses—often through delegation.

Decisive. After gathering information and involving other key people, the chief executive must be able to make decisions in a timely fashion. Whether it is a quiet, personal decision following private reflection or a group decision facilitated by the chief executive, the fundamental role of good leaders is to make the call.

Startup organizations are often managed by visionaries, who reach their goals by being flexible. As their organizations grow, however, no decision or a late decision has a negative effect. One way to compensate is to appoint a chief operating officer who makes decisions easily and put him or her in charge of daily operations. Then the strategic decisions are left to the chief executive, but routine decisions are someone else's responsibility.

PART 6

Organized or disciplined. Discipline in personal life carries over to discipline in organizational life. Well-organized chief executives know how to manage their schedules to keep family, friends, leisure, and work in balance. They manage their finances well enough to keep themselves and their organizations free from constant money crises. They track their work so they know when goals are reached. They delegate tasks that others can do as well or better.

A chief executive who is not well-organized needs a solid staff structure as a support and to get the day-to-day tasks accomplished.

Strategic. In the corporate world, buying, selling, merging, joint-venturing, subcontracting, and outsourcing are common practices because they increase profits. Nonprofits, too, can improve their bottom line by reaching out to other groups in the independent sector, to businesses, to media corporations, and to government agencies. They need a chief executive with the strategic vision, inventiveness, and diplomatic skills to bring together very different organizations to accomplish a shared goal.

Energetic. Chief executives always have new people to meet, literature to read, travel to schedule, and meetings to attend. If a chief executive is not naturally endowed with high energy, he or she must learn how to generate energy through proper exercise, diet, and rest and how to conserve energy through good planning, wise decision making, and a readiness to delegate.

Of course, this list of characteristics could go on and on; use it as a starting point for your own list of desired characteristics.

SUGGESTED ACTION STEPS

1. Board members, take inventory of your current chief executive. On a scale of 1 to 10, what rating would you give to each of the characteristics listed in this chapter? How can you enhance the greatest strengths?

2. Board chair, ask a few chief executives in the business world what characterizes success in their sector. How do those traits differ from success in the nonprofit community?

Q/A

70.

How do we find a new chief executive?

Whether the chief executive departs with little warning or provides one year's advance notice, the key steps in finding a replacement remain the same. All board members should participate in the following steps, which culminate with the full board voting on the final selection of the new chief executive.

Conduct a presearch assessment. The full board or executive committee should review the following:

- Mission and goals
- Staff morale and needs
- Current programmatic needs of the organization
- Constituency support
- Financial condition
- Previous chief executive's experience

Prepare a profile of desired characteristics. At a minimum, the board should sign off on a description of the desired competencies, character, personality, and experience a new chief executive should have (see Question 69). Even better, ask a number of people—including staff members, board members, major donors, and leaders in your sector—what characteristics a new chief executive should have for the current stage in the organization's lifecycle (see Question 71).

Define what the organization needs *before* you focus on particular candidates and their personalities. If your organization has been on a growth trajectory, for example, you might want to look for a chief executive who has experience leading a larger group. Or perhaps someone with a fundraising background would be a good fit, given the board's recent approval of a capital campaign case statement.

Write a position description. The chief executive of any organization is asked to achieve the intended results within the policy parameters set by the board. But candidates will want to see what the board expects the chief executive to accomplish, how the position relates to the board, and what the specific duties are. Take the time to write a new description that reflects the organization's current and evolving needs; don't simply use the current chief executive's job description.

Take care not to misrepresent the board's style in governing the organization or the job itself. A prospective chief executive must understand and agree with the board's expectations for how their roles work together to accomplish the organization's mission. If that doesn't happen, you will soon be conducting another executive search.

Manage the search. Form a committee to manage the search process and make recommendations to the board. Using a search committee invites wider participation, builds ownership in the decision, and allows board and staff to collaborate on a decision critical to both groups.

PART
6

The board must be clear in its mandate to the committee, providing a timetable, a budget, an explanation of its authority, and an idea of how many candidates to present to the board. Committee members are typically current or former board members, but they can also represent the organization's constituency and staff. The committee needs a coordinator to manage logistics, create candidate files, and organize committee meetings. This person must maintain strict confidentiality during the search.

Depending on the organization's size, complexity, and resources, some boards hire an executive search firm; they typically have national and international networks of candidates, and some even specialize in the nonprofit community. These firms, which generally charge a percentage fee based on the chief executive's compensation (plus expenses), provide an account executive to manage the search process.

An external search for a chief executive can easily take four or five months, or even longer in colleges or universities and other complex organizations where several constituencies must be involved and the search is national or international.

Identify candidates. Contacting a broad group of people who know good prospects is the primary way to build a list of potential candidates. A letter inviting nominations, sent to several hundred key constituents and leaders in the field by the board chair or the search committee chair, is well worth the effort. Often, top candidates are satisfied with their current jobs and are contacted because someone nominated them without their knowledge.

Well-placed ads can also help get the word out. As applicants and nominees become known, the search committee should send information on the organization's mission and goals and the desired qualifications of a new chief executive. Include a request for a letter of interest, a resume, and the names of references.

Don't be surprised if the candidates for the chief executive's position include a senior staff member or two. But even if the search committee suspects that an internal candidate might be the best choice for chief executive, it should complete all the steps in the search process; an even better candidate might surface along the way. Board members should fully expect the departure of any staff member who applies for the chief executive position but isn't selected.

Narrow the field. When the announced deadline is past, narrow the field to a short list of three to seven candidates who appear to meet the criteria set early in the process. (Never set an absolute deadline because you do not want to close out a good possibility.)

Call these individuals to ask whether they wish to be considered active candidates. Some of them may be happily situated in their current positions and need more information about what your organization has to offer. You want candidates who are drawn to your mission after studying your materials. And you should expect a challenge in winning the interest of some good nominees.

Conduct reference checks and interviews. Depending on time, distance, and funding, candidates on the short list typically are screened at length by phone after a few reference checks. Questions should be thoughtfully selected in advance and given to the search committee members who make the phone calls.

Arrive at the final two or three candidates after conducting a personal interview, several phone interviews, six to eight reference checks, and perhaps a credit check. Keep the process moving, but be thorough.

Negotiate with the selected candidate. The full board votes on the final selection, as recommended by the search committee. On behalf of the full board, the search committee should present a written offer. Give the candidate a few days to review the draft appointment document, which will be signed by both parties, and suggest changes. When the board and the new chief executive make verbal agreements, too many assumptions result and uncomfortable situations can later arise.

Announce the appointment and begin the transition. Once a decision has been made, contact those close to the organization, including key stakeholders and participants in the search process. Arrange for a special introduction to the staff and a press release. Once the decision is announced, the search coordinator should send letters to the other candidates, clean out and secure the files, pay outstanding bills, and write thank-you notes to all those who helped.

The board chair and a senior staff member should help ease the outgoing and new chief executives through the transition period. If the new chief executive is moving from another city, the appointment may not take effect for several months. In the interim, the new chief executive will want to be kept informed and be consulted on key issues before arriving for the first day of work. How the board and staff begin building their professional relationship with the new chief executive during this stage has a lot to do with his or her long-term success.

SUGGESTED ACTION STEPS

1. Board members, develop a policy on selecting a new chief executive now, before the need arises and as part of overall policymaking. It can be better thought out in calm than in crisis.

2. Board members, before beginning the search for a new chief executive, agree on which characteristics are essential to the position at this point in the organization's lifecycle.

PART
6

PART SEVEN

Organizational Change

Even when everything is going great for an organization, board members can't afford to become complacent. Change is always around the corner. The chief executive who has so expertly managed the organization's growth for several years may suddenly decide to retire. The base of donors that has been so stable over the past decade may start showing small cracks. Or maybe economic realities will dictate a different way of doing business.

If your organization waits for external change to occur, then reacts, it will forever be playing catch-up. But if the organization anticipates and prepares for external change, in addition to initiating internal change, it will be in a better position to fulfill its mission and realize its dreams.

Q
A

71.

What is the typical lifecycle for a nonprofit organization?

Nonprofit organizations often are categorized by the phase in their lifecycle. This evolutionary pattern clarifies the organization's capacity to deal with change, transitions, and crises. By understanding the kinds of challenges a young or a mature organization usually has to deal with, an organization may better learn how to overcome obstacles—or even better—prepare for them in a more constructive manner. The typical organizational lifecycle has five basic stages.

Startup. Many nonprofit organizations get started when a small group of people rallies around a common cause or a charismatic, visionary leader who can articulate what needs to be done and why. Read the histories of most nonprofits and you'll find stories of conversations around kitchen tables, chance encounters, and phone calls across town or across the country, all of which galvanized a group into action.

A sense of haphazardness, even controlled chaos, may characterize some groups in their early days, as people roll up their sleeves and do whatever needs to be done to fulfill and advance the mission. Board members may have hands-on management responsibilities in addition to oversight responsibilities, because most startup organizations rely completely on volunteers to accomplish the work.

Adolescence. In time, processes and procedures develop to ensure consistency as the ranks of volunteers expand. The organization becomes a legal entity, a board of directors is chosen, and programs and projects are formalized in a budget. Recognizing that they can't do it all, board members hire one staff member who, in turn, hires others. Revenues start to grow, and activities expand accordingly.

At this stage, it's important for the board to remove itself from operational issues and focus on strategic planning and the organization's long-term viability. It must put policies in place to provide stability to the organization as it experiences the highs and lows of the teenage years.

Adulthood. The organization grows in size, stature, and sophistication. Programs, procedures, and activities become formalized to the extent that staff, the board, constituents, and the public know what to expect from the organization. During this phase, organizations typically flourish—they have hit their stride.

By adulthood, the chief executive and the board have developed a clear understanding of their respective roles. The board naturally takes on more oversight responsibilities and becomes more sophisticated and proficient in fundraising and self-evaluation.

Old age. In this stage, the organization begins to show the wear and tear of being around for a while. It may have difficulty attracting board members or charitable contributions, experience a decrease in people using its services or buying its products, and see an increase in staff turnover (often accompanied by a decrease in staff morale). The general lack of enthusiasm about the organization may carry over to the board, resulting in lower participation in meetings and a greater tendency to rubber stamp decisions.

Death. The organization stops moving forward and stalls out, followed by a precipitous decline and probable closure. This stage typically is characterized by a poor perception of the organization among the public, a chief executive who is unwilling to make significant changes, and a board that is merely going through the motions of governing.

It is critical to remember that each of these stages can last a few months, a few years, or for the organization's entire existence. All five stages may never happen; some nonprofits skip a stage or two. It is perfectly acceptable for an organization to remain in one specific stage as long as it continues to pursue its mission and accomplish its desired work.

Combating Stagnation

If the board becomes too distant from its own responsibilities and the organization itself, stagnation may occur—of ideas, priorities, initiatives, leadership, and so forth. This can happen at any point in the lifecycle.

At the point of stagnation, however, a cycle of renewal can begin. If an organization monitors itself carefully and makes a commitment to taking action, it is possible for it to renew the vision and goals, change the direction of the downward curve, and begin another cycle of growth and energy. These situations are not necessarily the result of poor board or staff leadership; often, the world simply has changed faster than the organization.

Staying on top of emerging trends and shifts in the external environment can help a board steer the organization through the inevitable waves of change. When the needs of the communities, clients, or members served by the organization change—whether due to technological advances, world events, or socioeconomic developments—the organization must be prepared and positioned to change to remain relevant. As strategic opportunities present themselves, your organization can reshape its products, benefits, and services accordingly, reinventing itself in the process. Then stagnation never sets in.

PART
7

Although a natural part of the organizational lifecycle, renewal doesn't happen by chance. It takes courage and a positive, realistic philosophy. Sometimes organizational renewal calls for drastic action—for example, the dismissal of a chair who has served for twenty years or the release of the visionary founder who cannot see the need to change. Whatever it takes, it may be worth keeping the name, constituency, staff, and programs in place.

Is your organization due for renewal? That might be the case if it has already experienced the wobbly steps of infancy, the rapid growth associated with adolescence, and the stability of maturity. For example, if participation rates, revenue, staff turnover, and other important indicators are heading in the wrong direction, they signal the need for change—for adopting a "more youthful" outlook on the organization and how its mission can be accomplished.

Still, not all nonprofit organizations experience every stage of the typical lifecycle, nor does each stage last a particular number of years. An organization can zoom from infancy through adolescence in less than one year, then begin a rapid descent to closure before ever reaching full maturity. Conversely, years may pass before an organization finds its financial and programmatic footing and begins to develop into a confident and mature adult. Being aware of which lifecycle stage your organization is currently in will help you identify areas for improvement and potential growth.

SUGGESTED ACTION STEPS

1. Board chair, distribute a summary of the organizational lifecycle to board members and ask them to identify the organization's current location. Discuss the implications for governance.

2. Board members, identify the challenges inherent in the organization's stage, and discuss how the board can help the organization respond.

3. Chief executive, possibly as a prelude to the strategic planning process, invite a futurist to a board meeting for a presentation on emerging trends and their implications for the organization.

Q&A 72.

How do we ensure that the organization thrives after the founders depart?

At each stage of an organization's lifecycle (see Question 71), the potential for a leadership crisis exists. Making a smooth transition to the next stage calls for all volunteer leaders—not just the founders—to acknowledge the challenges of becoming older. At some point, others have to realize that they must become the bearers of the founders' vision and facilitate the renewal process—or watch the organization stumble through old age and eventually die.

The passion, creativity, and sheer energy that founders typically bring to an organization in its youth can propel it forward for years. But they will not always be around, whether by choice or by circumstance. What's essential is to have understandings and policies in place so that, when the day of departure arrives, both board and staff can continue to fulfill their respective roles without pause, with no one experiencing any hard feelings.

Here are some suggestions:

- *Reinforce the different roles.* If founders are also board members, they must remember to wear their "governance hat" to board meetings (see Question 2) and not become involved in operational details that, in the past, were near and dear to their hearts. The founders' emotional attachment to the organization complicates this task, requiring other board members to emphasize the delineation of board and staff responsibilities.

- *When appropriate, carve out a special role for the founders.* You might, for example, name them to an advisory council or engage their expertise in some other unique capacity (see Questions 18 and 33). Resist the temptation to create a "founder" position on the board. This puts the chief executive in the position of feeling as if every operational decision is second guessed or questioned and that his or her predecessor is also one of his or her "bosses."

- *Most important, establish clear guidelines and procedures.* Having board-approved systems in place ensures continuity when a transition occurs. The founders can feel secure knowing that the organization they worked so hard to create is still in good hands and will continue to do good work.

  In addition, established procedures help in situations in which the founders may have trouble letting go. Founders who must adhere to the same rules and standards as everyone else in the organization will not have the authorization to spend its money, enter into contracts, or hire and fire a chief executive without others' approval.

In the final analysis, no one owns a nonprofit organization. People will come and go over the years, with some leaving a bigger mark than others.

SUGGESTED ACTION STEPS

1. Chief executive, engage a volunteer to write or update the organizational history, to ensure that founders feel valued and acknowledged.

2. Board members, consider hiring a coach or consultant to work with each founder to develop a personal plan for how and when to leave the organization.

PART
7

73.

When should we enter into strategic alliances with other organizations?

Few organizations can do it all. Fewer still can afford it all. Surveying the economic landscape often leads boards to realize that it is futile to duplicate efforts when much can be gained by exploring partnership options with other nonprofits.

Strategic alliances can provide the essential leverage that helps nonprofit organizations fulfill their missions and expand the range of people they serve. These alliances can take a variety of forms: public-private partnerships, joint initiatives with organizations with similar missions, partnerships with community groups that reflect your actual or potential constituents, or contractual agreements with organizations that can help you deliver a service. Some alliances are purely financial in nature, whereas others can be programmatic or administrative.

Collaboration does not need to be complex. It could be as simple as splitting the salary of a shared staff member, the cost of a piece of equipment, or the use of a conference room. Two or more groups might form a purchasing group, jointly hire a legislative monitor, or even coordinate an event or program together. Each group maintains its autonomy and makes no commitment to working together again. This option provides an opportunity to learn about the other organization's culture and achieve some cost efficiencies, while gauging the willingness of both boards to explore a more formal strategic alliance.

In a more sophisticated partnership, the organizations might look into sharing administrative services, sharing office space, or launching several joint programs. Each group remains independent, but all partners begin to share the decision-making process and some systems.

In pursuing strategic alliances, nonprofit organizations must be open to departing from the status quo. This kind of change threatens many, including board members, so be sure to ask such strategic questions as the following:

- *What are our greatest assets?* With whom could we work to leverage them on behalf of more people? This will narrow the list of organizations that are good candidates for strategic partners. The chief executive should take the lead in reaching out to other organizations, but within parameters set by the board.

- *Will this alliance further our own mission?* A true partnership results when there is a true need for the service you want to provide and when real benefits accrue to all parties. Explore only those ideas that are win-win for all potential participants.

- *Do we and the proposed partner(s) have adequate staff and financial resources?* Foundations like to see collaboration, so consider obtaining seed money through foundation grants. Collaboration or partnership with for-profit corporations is certainly an option, with the caveat that the nonprofit should always retain control of its finances and never lose sight of its mission.

- *Is it the best way to achieve the desired results?* Set realistic goals and agree up front on criteria for measuring success. Be clear

PART
7

about what you gain out of this collaboration and where you need to compromise.

- *Are the added work and coordination time worth it?* You might want to try a pilot period, after which any organization can withdraw from the partnership with proper notice.

- *What are the governance implications?* They may be negligible or nonexistent. For example, if several nonprofits band together to form a purchasing group or hire a legislative advocate, yet maintain independent operations, their boards have to agree but do not have to intertwine.

SUGGESTED ACTION STEPS

1. Board members, appoint a task force to explore possible strategic alliances.

2. Board chair, ask eight to ten volunteers who know your organization but have no vested interest in it to brainstorm and come up with ten good ideas for strategic alliances. Take the list to the rest of the board for some "what if . . .?" discussion.

3. Board members, interview staff or board members from organizations that have entered into the kind of alliances you are considering. What have they learned?

Q&A

74.

When should we consider a merger or acquisition?

It's not just groups facing an economic downturn that look into the possibility of a merger. Heightened competition throughout the nonprofit sector—for top-notch staff, attractive benefits, political clout, media recognition, you name it—often prompts healthy, wealthy groups to seek partners with whom they can achieve even greater success.

Technically speaking, a merger involves two partners that agree to integrate their processes, programs, governance, and staff; a new name is often selected to reflect the fresh start being made by both groups. An acquisition refers to one organization gaining control of another and folding the latter into its own structure.

Before even mentioning the word *merger* in the same breath as another organization's name, consider collaborating in some way (see Question 73). If the partnership or alliance goes smoothly, thanks to similar missions, cultures, and goals, a merger might be an option down the road.

A merger involves restructuring both organizations and integrating all functions. For instance, merging your nonprofit with another is likely to require delicate negotiation regarding the number (and election process) of board members. You may need to set up a rotation system for the first few years to ensure that representatives of both groups have top leadership roles. Other key decisions—and possible sticking points—will involve staffing, finances, property and facilities, fundraising activities, programs, and services.

Key Considerations

Take the time to engage in serious debates about the pros and cons of a merger and in frank discussions about every detail of governance and operations. A board's failure to agree on these points in advance can seriously threaten the success of the new organization. Answering the following questions can help you clarify your organization's unique situation.

What is our goal? Do you seek organizational growth, a greater diversity of services, a wider geographic scope, a larger market, an enhanced public profile? All of those are valid reasons for a merger, as are realizing greater economies of scale and achieving a greater concentration on core competencies (doing more of what you do best).

If you are contemplating a merger because the organization may collapse financially without one, state that as well. This self-assessment should also include an honest appraisal of your organization's strengths and weaknesses, what makes it an attractive merger partner, and what the potential drawbacks are.

Poll all the board members, and you might be surprised by the range of responses. Only after leaders reach unity on organizational goals and agree on the results they expect from a merger can they approach another group at the negotiating table.

How compatible are our missions? Chances are, you are already aware of your potential partner's history, reputation, programs, and

PART
7

financial situation. Still, you'll need to conduct due diligence and thoroughly investigate the other group.

Be sure to pay attention to the other organization's mission. Is it similar to your own? Complementary? Even if the groups employ very different strategies, are they, at heart, focused on the same ends? Mergers can be challenging enough on their own; you need a mission on which both can agree to be the island in what may be a turbulent sea at times.

What do stakeholders think?   Conduct surveys and focus groups with the staff, community members, business leaders, funders, clients, customers, members, and so forth. Ask for their opinions on your organization's current situation, including its strengths and weaknesses. Identify concerns they may have about the organization potentially losing its identity through a merger or, conversely, what possibilities might open up if your group joined forces with another.

During the research phase, some groups find that, to the wider community, they are virtually indistinguishable from their competitors anyway so a merger would simply clear up existing confusion. Others discover emotions that run so deep that a merger would alienate key stakeholders. You won't know unless you ask.

What are the organizational cultures?   As objectively as possible, assess the values that guide the way each organization currently does business. Determine what your organization values and rewards (for instance, flexibility, risk taking, personal development, or cross-departmental initiatives). What is your perception of the other group? How manageable might the differences be?

Certainly each organization will have its own procedures and traditions where board and staff are concerned. Assuming that the bedrock beliefs that drive each group are similar, such as the mission, then any feelings of "us versus them" should subside given enough time and effort by all parties. Organizational experts say the best way to create a new culture is through communicating honestly and handling conflict (instead of avoiding it). Ideally, what emerges is a new culture entirely, one with its own traditions.

Who can help us through the process? An outside perspective is invaluable, especially when emotions run high in the boardroom and among staff members who don't know what's happening behind those closed doors. After all, a merger might mean that a chief executive, other employees, and some board members won't have roles within the new organization.

Hire an attorney or a consultant who has an expertise in nonprofit mergers. He or she will ask questions and raise important issues that might otherwise be ignored and can assist with developing an implementation timetable should the merger occur. Also appoint a merger negotiations committee with equal representation from both groups (including the chief executives) to work through the many issues.

One final caveat: mergers cost money. You'll need to pay attorneys, accountants, organizational consultants, printers, and information technology experts, to name just a few. You may need to craft an attractive severance package for your chief executive. In addition, there are the hidden costs, such as the time devoted by staff members to working out details, handling rumors, or simply being too distracted to do their jobs effectively. So if the motivating factor is short-term economic survival, broaden your perspective. A merger is for the long term.

SUGGESTED ACTION STEPS

1. Board chair, invite board chairs from similar types of organizations in your area to meet informally to discuss potential areas of collaboration or coordinated activities.

2. Board members, if a merger is a strong possibility for your organization, appoint a board-level task force to conduct due diligence on the other group and develop recommendations

for a smooth blending of the two staffs, cultures, and operational structures.

3. Board members, consider hiring a consultant to facilitate merger discussions and help bring the two groups together with minimal problems.

75.

How can we expand the organization's scope to an international level?

If your organization has a Web site, you are probably operating internationally whether you know it or not. The explosion of Internet usage throughout the world has opened the floodgates of information, enabling someone in Europe, Africa, or Asia to easily learn more about a U.S.-based organization—and vice versa. Time zones and geographical boundaries do not exist in cyberspace. In addition, the growth of multinational companies that provide the same products and services in numerous countries and the fact that air travel has become commonplace have increased people's comfort level. What's foreign is no longer strange or unknown.

That said, moving an organization with a local, regional, or national scope to the international arena has numerous implications. Simply adding the words *international* or *global* to your organization's name and mission statement won't do the trick. A truly international organization operates with a global mind-set and culture. It becomes second nature for such a group to take into account the worldwide implications of every decision made or every activity undertaken.

Key Considerations

Expanding into international activities may not be a logical extension of your organization's mission statement. In that case, the board should analyze whether the potential for operating internationally is even worth pursuing. Or perhaps the mission needs to be revisited and revised (see Question 4).

The direction to expand globally must not only come from the board but also enjoy its full support. Consider the following questions, which can help your board frame the do-we-or-don't-we discussion.

What would the organization and its stakeholders gain? If your organization already enjoys high market penetration, it's only natural to look to other countries where people might be eager to purchase your products and services, attend your meetings and shows, even pay dues or make contributions to support your efforts. Your organization may not have competitors in some geographic areas, positioning it as the sole provider of solutions to people's unmet needs.

More is at stake, however, than a bigger organizational bank account. You may have key constituents whose own businesses or organizations would benefit from an entry into international markets—you could pave the way for those unable to make headway on their own. Or you may represent people with a vested interest in how international standards and policies are set for various sectors of the economy.

International activity is not a one-way street. Don't forget what your organization may be able to learn from abroad when it comes to fundraising, influencing public policy, program development, leadership development, or community service. Initiatives that succeed in one country can, possibly with a few tweaks, prove just as effective somewhere else. Widening your perspective can enrich your organization's culture and operations.

PART
7

Another potential gain comes in the form of recognition as a good global citizen. Many U.S.-based organizations have undertaken international programs aimed solely at helping people in need—of medical attention, food, clothing, books, shelter, and educational materials. Although they sometimes require delicate negotiations with foreign governments, these humanitarian efforts are typically well-received by all parties involved.

What would the organization and its stakeholders lose? As alluring as the promise of increased revenues can be, the old saying holds true: it takes money to make money. Devoting dollars to support an international expansion will probably mean shifting money away from an established program. Not spending the money, however, might lead to a loss of market share or a diminished reputation as a leader or authority in the field.

What are the staffing implications? An organization can begin exploring the international arena without a dedicated staff in place, and can even generate revenues by tapping new markets and audiences. For a global mind-set to be integrated throughout the organization, however, the board must make a statement by issuing a policy that designates the position responsible. At a minimum, one staff member must be dedicated to developing and implementing any international initiatives.

What are the governance implications? Just like their domestic counterparts, international stakeholders will want a voice within the organization. Including board members from other countries may require a bylaws amendment, not to mention adjustments in how the board communicates, when and how it meets, how board orientation is handled, what is expected of each member, and so forth.

You'll also need to consider how to develop future leaders from afar and how to keep them involved in committee or task force activities. This, in particular, will require an awareness and acceptance of cultural differences and customs. As a whole, the board must have the patience and flexibility to adapt its structure and functioning to welcome members from outside its traditional circles.

What legal issues may arise? Many nonprofit organizations based in the United States enjoy tax-exempt status; they aren't required to pay taxes on revenue generated by activities related to their tax-exempt purpose. That's not necessarily the case elsewhere. In other countries, for instance, your organization may have to pay tax on electronic transactions, sales of products and services, meetings or conventions, membership dues, or even charitable contributions. Also, international financial transactions can be cumbersome, differing from country to country and depending on the international agreements the United States has with a specific nation.

Intellectual property is an especially hot issue. Other countries don't take the same approach as the United States does to protect copyrights and trademarks. You may have little recourse if an organization based abroad helps itself to your Web-based content. Consult with an attorney who is well-versed in international law.

How can we overcome communication challenges? Given the widespread acceptance of English throughout the world, language may not present a large barrier. Much will depend on the prevailing customs within your organization's field. Within some medical circles, for instance, English is the accepted language and therefore translations aren't necessary. However, some international groups designate several official languages.

With whom might we partner? Expanding your scope of operations across the Atlantic or Pacific doesn't necessarily mean flying solo. In fact, you might be able to make inroads faster, less expensively, or more effectively by aligning with other organizations that share your values but have a better understanding of cultural contexts. For instance, the board might vote to cosponsor activities with international affiliates or sister organizations or enter into a partnership agreement with a for-profit or nonprofit entity.

PART
7

Ways to Globalize

Small steps taken toward globalization can lead to a leap forward in your organization's name recognition, reputation, and overall value. These steps might include the following:

- *Study similar organizations that have registered success with global initiatives.* Discuss their strategies.
- *Establish chapters or affiliates overseas.* Typically, each chapter or affiliate operates autonomously while adhering to organizational guidelines (such as mission, code of ethics, financial reporting, and so forth).
- *Attend meetings with board members from your international counterparts.* Look for ways your organizations can work together to address similar issues or interests.
- *Revise the governance structure to encourage wider participation.* Board meetings via audio or teleconference may make more sense for directors scattered across time zones, although state laws probably require at least one face-to-face meeting annually. Consider forming an international advisory council (see Question 18).
- *Organize a board study mission abroad.* When board members meet face to face with their counterparts in other countries, they will better understand global challenges and opportunities.

SUGGESTED ACTION STEPS

1. Board chair, schedule a brainstorming session for board members to discuss the implications of expanding into international markets or programs.
2. Board members, appoint a task force of board and staff members to research what steps, either large or small, your organization can take toward globalization.

Q A

76.

Should our charitable organization engage in lobbying?

True or false: the law forbids a 501(c)(3) organization from engaging in activities aimed at influencing legislation—what's commonly known as lobbying.

The statement is false. Within limits, a charitable organization *can* engage in lobbying. In fact, many more organizations could increase their impact by carefully undertaking lobbying activities. What they can't engage in is electioneering—getting involved in supporting or opposing a particular political candidate. (Incidentally, get-out-the-vote and voter education campaigns are not considered electioneering.) Many fewer restrictions apply to 501(c)(6) associations and 501(c)(4) social welfare organizations, which, for example, may devote their main efforts to lobbying and may disburse funds to specific candidates through political action committees (PACs). At the other end of the spectrum, private foundations cannot engage in any type of lobbying or political activity.

PART
7

Lobbying policymakers is just one aspect of political or social involvement. Another is advocacy, which is simply arguing in favor of a particular cause or action. By their very existence, nonprofit organizations are advocates for something specific, whether it's the arts, the environment, education, and so forth. And one of the responsibilities of a board member is to support and speak in favor of the organization itself, at every opportunity.

When advocacy becomes more intense and directed toward legislators or even the general public, it can turn into lobbying. The Internal Revenue Service (IRS) recognizes two categories of lobbying:

- *Direct lobbying* involves direct contact between legislators and an organization. It refers to specific legislation, communicates the organization's strong preference or firm position on that legislation, and guides the legislator to vote in a certain manner.

- *Grassroots lobbying* is directed at the general public and includes a "call to action" for the public to contact their legislative body about a specific piece of legislation. This type of lobbying also communicates a particular position or preference for or against the legislation.

To be considered lobbying, an activity must meet all of the criteria outlined in the definitions. For example, informing a segment of the public about a piece of legislation without issuing a specific call to action would not fulfill the definition of grassroots lobbying.

Remember, it is well within their rights for charitable organizations to engage in either direct or grassroots lobbying. The only restriction, according to the IRS, is that lobbying cannot represent a "substantial part" of the organization's overall activities. Because the IRS has not defined "substantial," many nonprofits shy away from lobbying altogether and therefore miss out on opportunities to influence policymakers' decisions.

A better choice for the organization might be to avoid the ambiguity and submit to the lobbying expenditure test as outlined in

Section 501(h) of the Internal Revenue Code. Under the 501(h) option, a charitable organization cannot spend more than 20 percent of its first $500,000 of exempt expenditures on lobbying. In total, expenditures related to lobbying cannot top $1 million, with no more than 25 percent of those expenditures devoted to grassroots lobbying. The 501(h) option tallies actual money and staff time spent on lobbying, which the organization is probably tracking anyway, so it's an easier path to exercising influence over issues of concern.

Note, however, that funds obtained through federal grants cannot be spent on lobbying activities.

Lobbying doesn't have to be a big-dollar activity that takes place only in statehouses and on Capitol Hill. Depending on your organization's scope, you can seek to influence decisions made by members of city councils or regional boards.

SUGGESTED ACTION STEPS

1. Chief executive, invite a legal expert to give a presentation on how the organization can participate in government relations activities without jeopardizing its tax-exempt status.

2. Board members, appoint a task force of board and staff members to research whether it would be beneficial for the organization to participate in a coalition or legislative monitoring program with other organizations that have similar positions on issues.

77.

How should we respond to an organizational emergency or controversy?

Any number of crises can beset a nonprofit. They may fall into the "Acts of God" category (hurricane, tornado, flood) or represent a tragic occurrence (loss of human life). These types of emergency situations require an immediate response and obvious action on the part of the organization. Depending on the type and severity of the emergency, the response will vary. Should the headquarters office be ruined by fire or flood waters, for example, the organization should have a recovery plan in place that outlines how the organization can continue to function while returning to near-normal operations as soon as possible. A recovery plan for coping with the sudden death of the chief executive would contain different elements.

Other crisis situations raise controversy or affect the organization's reputation by attracting negative media coverage. These types of crises often have financial or personal elements, or both—for example, a board chair who becomes embroiled in a corporate scandal or a senior staff member who embezzles from the organization. They also require an effective response, as well as sensitivity to protecting the organization's image and reputation. When such controversies arise, it's best to have one spokesperson, who has been trained in dealing with the media, to handle the tough questions adroitly and honestly.

The best time to address crisis management is when all is calm, when board members can objectively focus on ideal practices. Following are three steps to get started.

Review what has happened to other nonprofit groups. Consider problems such as natural disasters, terrorist attacks, or financial debacles to spark a board discussion on the potential economic, technical, and operational crises the organization should be prepared to address. After coming up with a list of potential crises, the board should identify the top ten issues the organization might possibly face.

Develop "what if" scenarios for the five most critical issues on the list. Have the board talk through how the organization should respond in each instance. For example, what steps should the organization take to get back to business as usual following the devastation of a natural disaster? How should the organization respond if an attendee is assaulted during one of its programs? What should the organization do if the board discovers that a large sum of money is missing?

Develop policies to address the various types of crises that are most likely to occur. These will form an overall crisis management plan that can be tweaked depending on the circumstances. The policies should address such questions as the following:

- *Who will serve as the "commander in chief" if an emergency occurs or a controversy erupts?* Having a command hierarchy in place will reduce confusion because board members already know where they should focus their individual efforts.

PART
7

- *Who is allowed to speak on behalf of the organization?* Your policies should outline who responds on behalf of the organization and how communications with various audiences—both external and internal—are handled. In some organizations the board chair serves as the spokesperson; other organizations rely on the chief executive or public relations director to fill that role. Another option is to designate several spokespeople, each qualified to speak about a different aspect of the crisis or controversy but all working under the direction of the person in charge of the organizational response.

- *What information is considered public, and therefore available for release to the media, and what is considered private?* Your attorney can address what information might raise legal liability concerns.

- *Who has the responsibility of calling a press conference?* Your organization, for instance, may sanction only those press conferences organized by the chief spokesperson.

- *What is the organization's responsibility should serious injury or death result?* For example, your policy may include paying for funeral expenses and expressing public condolences, when appropriate.

- *How often should the crisis management policies be reviewed and revised?* Establishing a regular schedule for reviewing the policies will keep board members aware of the potential for a crisis at any time.

Remember that anything related to your organization's external or internal affairs can become the target of media scrutiny, from actions of board and staff members to incidents within the field or profession. Even if those incidents occur elsewhere, reporters may contact your organization looking for a local angle. How you respond can negate years of good public relations work, or better position your organization for favorable coverage in the future.

SUGGESTED ACTION STEPS

1. Board members, designate board and staff members to serve as members of the crisis-management team.

2. Board members, ensure that the organization has an updated crisis management plan in place.

3. Board members, arrange for the board chair or other designated spokesperson to be provided with media training that includes mock interviews and press conferences.

78.

When should a nonprofit hire a consultant?

Most organizations need to retain a consultant from time to time to help either board members or staff members with their respective duties. Even if board members could do the task as well, the politics of some situations, or the lack of time to focus on the task, might suggest the need for one or more consultants. To avoid additional conflicts of interest, use the consultant as an outside hired expert; don't elect him or her to serve on the board if you plan to use his or her services on a contractual basis.

Many lawyers, accountants, and other types of consultants specialize in the nonprofit sector. They bring specialized skill, as well as experience and a network of contacts gained from working with other nonprofits. Perhaps most important, they are objective, outside observers, with no vested interests in your organization. That enables them to provide frank feedback and a fresh perspective on the situation. The information and ideas they offer can help your organization long after the consulting period has ended.

Consider retaining an outside consultant to assist the board with

- Strategic planning
- A search for a new chief executive
- A comprehensive fundraising program or capital campaign
- Monitoring of trends or legislation that could have an effect on future strategies
- Preventive legal services, legal audits, and legal defense
- Accounting systems, financial audits, and investment strategies

SUGGESTED ACTION STEPS

1. Board members, consider whether the full board could benefit from outside counsel. Think in terms of the value received in light of your mission and total budget.

2. Chief executive, look into sharing a consultant (and the accompanying expenses) with another nonprofit organization.

PART
7

79.

When should the board consider closing a nonprofit organization?

Like small businesses in the for-profit world, most new nonprofits do not last beyond five years. Most plan to, but circumstances lead them to close. It is more newsworthy when a nonprofit organization that is fifty to seventy-five years old decides to shut its doors. Perhaps a few critical decisions here and there, an infusion of cash at the right time, or the arrival of a new leader who renews the enthusiasm of the stakeholders could have held off the inevitable in some situations.

But the birth and death of organizations are parts of their lifecycle (see Question 71). There are always new visions and new energetic leaders ready to make their mark on society.

Board members usually know intuitively when the organization has moved from energy, growth, and vision to maintenance, defensiveness, and a sinking-ship mentality. At that point, one or more board members should suggest looking at the options while they remain viable. They must exercise acts of leadership, such as opening a dialogue with other organizations' leaders and considering a merger.

What doesn't work is choosing to ignore the writing on the wall or simply hoping that a miracle will occur. If a board evaluates and monitors itself honestly (see Question 47), members will know when the time has come to close down the organization. Then they will celebrate the good the organization has accomplished, pay off creditors, give the staff ample notice, and leave with all heads held high.

While the organization is still healthy, the board should agree on what the signs will be that it should plan to shut down. These signs should be relevant to each organization, measurable, and both subjective and objective. Examples might include a minimum number of staff members that can be supported, the depletion of reserve funds, or a drop in donors by more than 40 percent from the peak year. Having such concrete benchmarks prevents board members from thinking that such serious problems are only short term.

When the time for closing is imminent, bring in an attorney and a CPA to help the organization shut down its operations. Be honest with donors and beneficiaries, most of whom will respect the candor. If the organization closes soon enough, there may be some funds left over—after bills are paid and staff members receive appropriate severance—to pass along to a similar organization. The infusion of capital might allow that organization to continue serving some of your constituents or to hire a few members of your staff.

Board members' responsibilities do not end until all legal and human aspects of closing have been addressed. Their oversight of the organization continues until all of the closing steps have been completed, all of the staff members have been appropriately compensated, all of the liabilities have been handled, and all of the assets distributed. Finally, the board should host one last gathering to say good-bye to one another and to the organization.

SUGGESTED ACTION STEPS

1. Board members, if most of you agree that your organization is faltering, schedule a board retreat or assign a task force to define what needs to be done to change the downward curve into a new phase of renewal.

2. Board members, if your organization might be on its last leg, quietly seek counsel in designing an honorable plan for closing the shop.

3. Board chair, assign someone to gather information on how and why organizations similar to yours terminated operations.

PART
7

$\mathcal{QA}$ 80.

How does the board keep up with organizational change?

As your organization evolves, the board should evolve with it. Whether the change is monumental or modest, the board should closely track those changes. While it sounds risky to constantly change your board practices, you actually risk more by doing nothing. The "bored board" lacks meaningful engagement. These boards provide little oversight and can muddle organizational vision. Nonprofits that succeed in ever-more-demanding times expand their expectations of their boards' contributions to match their changing operational context. The boards that adjust and adapt help their organizations remain nimble and bring leadership, continuity, and vision to their missions.

   As you go through leadership rituals and routines—as board members and executive staff—take the opportunity to challenge your governance assumptions and redesign your board practices. Follow these five simple guidelines:

   1. *Be attentive*. Governance demands board attention. Accountability is the watch word of the day, and it requires that

compliance and performance go hand in hand. In a world filled with nonprofits struggling for survival and newspaper reports of governance gaffs, an engaged board is dedicated to the organization's mission, knowledgeable about the organization's goals and finances, committed to securing necessary financial resources, and capable of representing the organization in the community.

2. *Be honest.* At the heart of nonprofit leadership is the relationship between the board and the chief executive. The chief executive must be more than competent and confident. He or she also must be frank, open, and honest with the board. The board, in turn, must be supportive of the chief executive and committed to ensuring success. As interlocking pieces in a jigsaw puzzle that together create a complete picture, the chief executive and the board are complements, with mutual trust, respect, and appreciation building the foundation for a leadership team that can handle short-term and long-term challenges.

3. *Be intentional.* As Cyril Houle said, "A good board is a victory, not a gift." Great governance doesn't just happen by accident. It takes the right people in the right place at the right time. Who's on a board matters, and board composition is an important factor in organizational success. Good nonprofit leadership is thoughtful, self-aware, and proactive. It balances the need for long-term stability with the need to adapt its own structures and practices as circumstances change and the organization evolves.

4. *Be flexible.* Leadership should be agile. To realize its true potential, the board needs to be aware of its governance strategies and adjust them accordingly. The world around us has changed dramatically in the last few decades, with funding streams, public policy, politics, technology, demographics, the economy, and community needs constantly evolving. Most likely, your organization has also changed in big and little ways over the years.

Board structures, practices, and behaviors—whether explicit or implicit—need to be reviewed and updated to ensure that they remain relevant and appropriate. Likewise, the board needs to be flexible in its approach to leadership and decision making, adjusting its practices to the situation at hand. Reviewing the auditor's report is a different kind of activity than relocating the office—both demand special attention and tactics.

5. *Be productive*. Boards have a tendency toward talk rather than action. Demand, drive for, and deliver results. The board represents raw material that can, if used properly, have incredible impact. But board work is just that, work. It requires more than mere attendance at meetings. It requires of board members personal motivation and commitment, intellectual curiosity and challenge, and a passion for the organization's cause. In turn, the chief executive must be ready, willing, and able to engage board members in making sense of situations, in determining what matters, and in solving dilemmas. Neither the board nor the chief executive can simply go through the governance motions and expect great results.

SUGGESTED ACTION STEPS

1. Chief executive, inform the board of your needs as the administrator of the organization, and engage board members collectively and individually in addressing important issues.

2. Board members, follow changes in the external environment that have an impact on your organization and community, and discuss these changes during meetings.

3. Board members and chief executive, be aware of the internal changes that influence organizational management and governance, and respond to these changes with creativity and courage.

PART
7

Conclusion

Nonprofit organizations differ in size, structure, and complexity, but the elements of good governance are constant. A board may meet every legal requirement and adhere to proper procedures and still be ineffective if it is not engaged in setting strategic direction and supporting the organization. If a board neglects the full range of its responsibilities, it may preclude the organization from reaching its potential.

Good governance is about providing critical capital—intellect, reputation, resources, and access—to strengthen the organization and, in turn, the community it serves. An exceptional board recognizes the impact of its leadership, and board members understand that they must be thoughtful and engaged leaders, not competent but passive stewards.

Lessons Learned

Dedicated to increasing the effectiveness of nonprofit organizations by strengthening their boards of directors, BoardSource has worked with thousands of nonprofit board members and executives over the course of twenty years. We have encountered talented board members who were constrained by their limited board roles. We have seen "bored boards" that were underutilized or whose talents were going to waste. We have heard from nonprofit executives who had to prod board members to make good on their promises. Through these encounters, we have learned a few lessons about the value and challenges of good governance:

- *Board work and governance are not synonymous.* Boards govern, but that is not all that they do. They brainstorm and trouble-shoot, they cheer and salute the good work of the staff, and they raise money and open doors. And while governance is presumed to be the purview of boards, it is also the domain of other entities. Conscientious chief executives, demanding funders and attentive donors, government agencies and regulatory bodies all perform monitoring and oversight. These forces are part of an interlocking governance function that helps hold the nonprofit accountable. However, the board still retains—and cannot abdicate—ultimate responsibility for the organization. Organizations and chief executives need boards that do all of these things and often more. The challenge is being clear about what the task at hand is, then deciding how best to dispense with it.

- *Money is left—figuratively and literally—on the boardroom table.* Boards represent an underutilized resource for nonprofit organizations. Staff members yearn for the triumvirates of W's and T's—"wealth, wisdom, and work" and "time, talent, and treasure." The potential is obvious, but real value remains elusive. Of course, board members are expected to contribute—and contribute generously—cold, hard cash. But by reshaping our notion of board member contributions and adjusting our thinking about board composition, we might also be able to tap into the intangible resources that board members bring to the organization. Boards should be encouraged to think creatively. They can reframe questions that define an organization's future. When boards are free to be innovative, they go beyond oversight and into leadership.

- *When the board shoe doesn't fit, find another.* One size does not fit all boards, and boards can and should change. Governance practices and structures should be neither superimposed nor static. In encountering boards that broke with convention—paying board members, abolishing term limits, having staff members on the board—we found boards that took time for reflection and refinement. These boards defined their own culturally appropriate norms that facilitated buy-in and engagement. There's no single blueprint for a board's success. Nonprofit leaders must consider their own organizations' history and values.

As you evaluate your own practices, please keep in mind that the answers in this book do not address the complexities of each individual situation. No organization should blindly follow the lead of others. Sometimes discrepancies in behavior can be a good thing, especially when they result from a thoughtful evaluation of the needs of your nonprofit. Conformance, at times, can give an organization a false sense of confidence and conviction that it is doing the right thing.

The objective of *The Nonprofit Board Answer Book* is to give you a starting point from which to build your own practices. We encourage you to take note of the practices of others in the nonprofit world and then to look at your board and evaluate your organization based on its constituents and organizational needs. A discussion with your board about the practices of other organizations might highlight ways to improve your own practices. For sure, this effort is worthwhile. After all, effective boards are one of the keys to effective organizations.

Index